RUSKIN POTTERY

Self-portrait of Edward Richard Taylor, the founder of the Ruskin Pottery, with a range of Ruskin wares made by him and his son, William Howson Taylor.

RUSKIN POTTERY

The pottery of Edward Richard Taylor and William Howson Taylor, 1898 - 1935

Paul Atterbury & John Henson

Photography by Graham Miller

Baxendale Press 1993

ACKNOWLEDGEMENTS

The inspiration to write this book came from four great Ruskin enthusiasts, Miles and Adam Ferneyhough, Albert Wade and Richard Dennison, and the authors are grateful for their help and support at all stages. Particular thanks are also due to the individuals who contributed in so many ways to the successful preparation and production of the book, namely Audrey Atterbury, Maureen Batkin, Victoria Bergesen, John Cola, Richard Dennis, Susan Gordon, Don Hall, Jennifer Kavanagh, Tatiana Marsden, Mark Newstead, Jennifer Opie, James Ruston and Sue Whitaker.

The staff of many museums have been patient and helpful with the authors' interminable enquiries, notably Stella Beddoe (Keeper of Decorative Arts, Brighton), E Myra Brown (Curator of Ceramics, Liverpool) Patricia Collins (Curator of Ceramics, Burrell Collection, Glasgow), Ruth Denison (Curator, Coalport Museum), Samantha Flavin (Curatorial Assistant, Leeds), Lesley Jackson (Acting Senior Keeper, Decorative Arts, Manchester), A Moszynski (Ironbridge Gorge Museum), Kathy Niblett (Senior Assistant Keeper of Ceramics, Stoke-on-Trent), Helen Spencer (Assistant Keeper, Applied Art Department, Birmingham), Francesca Wagstaff (Curatorial Assistant, Wednesbury), Karin Walton (Curator of Applied Arts, Bristol) and Pamela Wood (Nottingham Castle Museum).

The majority of the photographs were taken specially by Graham Miller, whose own enthusiasm for the products and philosophies of the Arts and Crafts movement is apparent in the results. Additional photographs were taken or supplied by Victoria Bergesen, Christie's, Miles and Adam Ferneyhough, Glen Bank Photography, Bob Gordon, James Ruston, Sandwell Metropolitan Borough Council, Sotheby's, Bob Wallis Studio and Gerald Wells, Northern Counties Photographers.

The design and production of a complicated book has been turned from a pain into a pleasure by the ever-friendly staff of Flaydemouse.

Finally, special thanks are due to Caroline de Lane Lea for tolerating for so many years the invasive demands of the Ruskin book.

© Paul Atterbury and John Henson, 1993

Produced in Great Britain by Flaydemouse, Yeovil, Somerset

Published by the Baxendale Press, 1993

Distributed by Richard Dennis Publishing, The Old Chapel,
Shepton Beauchamp, Ilminster, Somerset TA19 0LE
Telephone: 0460 42009

ISBN 0 9520933 0 8

British Library Cataloguing-in-Publication Data
A catalogue record for this book is available from the British Library

CONTENTS

Above: William Howson Taylor as a child, painted by his father.
Below: The soufflé glazed display letters from the façade of the Ruskin Pottery.

INTRODUCTION

'Tis opportune to look back upon old times, and contemplate our forefathers. Great examples grow thin, and to be fetched from the passed world. Simplicity flies away, and iniquity comes at long strides upon us. We have enough to do to make up ourselves from present and passed times, and the whole stage of things scarse serveth for our instruction.'

Sir Thomas Browne, *Urne Buriall*

This book is a celebration of the work of two great potters of the past, Edward Richard Taylor and William Howson Taylor, father and son, who together with their craftsmen and women created some of the finest pottery that has ever been made. They named their factory the Ruskin Pottery in honour of the great writer and critic, John Ruskin. In the period since the closure of the factory, now more than 50 years, critical opinion has tended to favour, in Britain certainly, a more decorative style than that of the Taylors but in the period in which it was made the pottery enjoyed a worldwide reputation.

The story of the factory is a fascinating one, but William Howson Taylor, by nature reserved, would endorse the view that it is only the pots which matter. It is upon these that our closest attention should be focused, while at the same time endeavouring to understand adequately the influences and personalities which led to their manufacture and to the form which they took.

When the Ruskin Pottery was established in 1898 Britain had the largest empire ever known and was by far the largest exporter of manufactured goods, but the advantage of this dominant position in world trade was being challenged by America and Germany. It would have been impossible at that time to conceive of the extent to which British fortunes were going to deteriorate by the close of the pottery in 1935.

The cultural significance of this surplus of wealth, albeit in a few hands, was to enable a flourishing manufacture of works of art and craft. Much, or even most, of what was produced was traditional and historical in conception. The Ruskin Pottery as will be seen, fitted perfectly into this artistic, commercial and social pattern. The middle of the 1900s saw a period of depressed trading in Britain which seems to have affected the arts and crafts industries particularly badly. In the pre-First World War period the Ruskin Pottery looked to overseas markets, especially to the rich and expanding one of the USA. With the apparent decline in British sales after 1910 export markets became all-important for the pottery, and this factor determined its status in the war period. The immediate aftermath of the war was a boom which lasted from about March 1919 to April 1920. In 1921 a world depression set in, and in Britain the resulting recession forced many out of business. Trade protectionism began to increase, with heavy duties imposed by many countries on imported goods.

From the mid-1920s most western countries, except Britain, enjoyed a boom in production, but it was short-lived. By 1927 the American economy was also showing signs of a slow-down which the financial markets ignored, a situation which eventually led to the financial crises of 1929. The Ruskin Pottery was finally affected by all this economic turbulence, but when William Howson Taylor decided to close it in 1933, his reasons were more personal than financial.

Throughout its existence the pottery was, as a result, able to maintain its particular spirit of independence, thanks largely to the single-mindedness of the Taylors, father and son. Determined from the outset to produce exactly the kind of pottery they wanted, the Taylors were essentially products of the British Arts and Crafts movement. Historically, this movement was the creation of two distinct generations. The older generation, to which Edward Taylor belonged, was born in the period 1830-1845, while the younger generation was born in the period 1855-1870. William Howson Taylor, Edward Taylor's youngest child, was born in 1876 and so was among the younger followers of Arts and Crafts philosophies. The main period of the Arts and Crafts movement in Britain covered the 75 years from the founding of Morris, Marshall, Faulkner and Company in 1861 to the mid-1930s.

The careers of Edward and William Howson Taylor span this main period, from the appointment of Edward Taylor to the Birmingham Municipal School of Art in 1878 to the final closure of the Ruskin Pottery in 1935. The pottery itself came somewhat late onto the scene but its early years coincided with the period of the most intense artistic activity in Birmingham. John Ruskin, born in 1819 and therefore significantly older than the other members of the Arts and Crafts movement, can be seen as the founding father, taking precedence in time as well as in the formulation of the philosophy behind the movement. However, the key figure in the interpretation of Ruskin's work in relation to the Arts and Crafts movement as it developed in the years from 1871 was William Morris. Thus, directly relevant was the influence of Morris on the Taylors and the point at which that influence began. Edward Taylor took up his appointment at the Birmingham School of Art at the same time as Morris began an important series of lectures which were published in 1882 in a volume entitled 'Hopes and Fears for Art; Five lectures delivered in Birmingham, London and Nottingham 1878 – 81'. In 1880 Morris was made the new President of the Birmingham Society of Arts, and it was from this date that the School of Art and the teaching methods employed there by Edward Taylor began to enjoy a reputation that spread far beyond the boundaries of Birmingham.

Giving evidence to the Royal Commissioners on Technical Instruction in March 1882, Morris said that 'beauty is a marketable quality and ... the better the work is all round, both as a work of art and in its technique, the more likely it is to find favour with the public.' This was undoubtedly the marketing philosophy of both Morris & Company and the Ruskin Pottery.

There are many parallels between the workshops of Morris & Company, especially at Merton Abbey, and the Ruskin Pottery, though neither could be considered especially close to the Ruskinian ideals. When it came to working practices there was a considerable difference between theory and practice, as William Morris acknowledged. Although not a potter himself, Morris set out guidelines for the art potter, following Ruskinian principles. These stated that articles should not be moulded if they could be made on the wheel or in some other way by hand, that pottery should not be decorated by printing, and painting should be confined to what can only be done on pottery, that pottery should not be finished by turning on the lathe, and that excessive neatness was undesirable, especially for cheap wares. In broad terms the guidelines were followed at the Ruskin Pottery, and the Taylors echoed them in the introduction to their 1905 catalogue. At the same time, the two organisations had much in common in their working practices, namely that the workers made up the designs of their employers and were not allowed to deviate significantly from them, that technical knowledge was restricted to what was necessary for the employee to know, that the division of tasks was well-defined, that there was no individual recognition for the employees with all products bearing only the company name, that no modern machinery was used that reduced employees to the level of operatives, and that rates of pay and conditions of work were better than those found usually in the industry. In fact, Howson Taylor came far closer to Ruskinian ideals than Morris or his father in his relationship with his employees.

Inspired as it was by the principles of both John Ruskin and William Morris, the Ruskin Pottery could be seen as the perfect example of an Arts and Crafts industry. Deliberately small in scale, its well-treated employees produced over a long period individual objects of great beauty and high quality, aimed at a specific and exclusive sector of the market, objects that could be seen as luxuries designed simply to enhance the lives, and the homes, of those who bought them. In the process the Taylors, like William Morris, seem to have run a profitable business. Considering the times in which it operated, the Ruskin Pottery was a remarkably successful art industry.

Chapter I
ORIENTAL AND EUROPEAN INFLUENCES

The one important element that links together so much of William Howson Taylor's Ruskin Pottery is its orientalism and its dependence specifically upon Chinese shapes and glazes. On one level it is possible to interpret Howson Taylor's pottery, along with much of the output of his Arts and Crafts contemporaries, as merely a continuation of the stylistic love affair with the Orient that had played so dominant a role in European art and design since the 17th century. The English enthusiasm for chinoiserie in the 18th century came into England, not directly from the Far East, but indirectly via Holland and France. In the 19th century the cult of Japanism, which swept across England from the 1860s, followed a similar pattern, with France once again setting the style. Although the passion for Japanese art and design was all powerful during the 1870s and 1880s in Britain, the traditional role of China as the primary inspirational source for European ceramics was never completely overshadowed. As a result, in the latter part of the 19th century the defining boundaries between Chinese and Japanese art and design became increasingly blurred. By the late 1870s the universal appeal of decorative French-inspired Japanism had ensured that its powerful symbolism had been steadily debased by the manufacturers of cheap teapots and mass-produced wallpapers, but at the same time, this popularity has to be seen against the background of renewed enthusiasm for Chinese art. The cult of blue and white porcelain was a well-documented phenomenon of the period, thanks to the trend established by Whistler, Rossetti and their circles, and its impact can be measured by cartoons in *Punch* and the Gilbert and Sullivan operetta *Patience*. However, the success of the blue and white style was matched by widespread ignorance about what collectors were actually buying. Oriental connoisseurship was in its infancy, and few collectors could tell the difference between Ming blue and white copies made in the 17th, 18th or even 19th centuries. Some were even unaware of the distinctions between Chinese and Japanese porcelains. Examples of famille rose, famille verte, famille noire and other export porcelains were also collected in an equally indiscriminate way. It was the style that counted, not pedantic concerns about age and authenticity. The natural result of this was a general enthusiasm for orientalism *per se*, with considerable Sino-Japanese style confusion. Many of the wares produced by both industrial and art potters

during this period reflect this muddle, with a notable example being Minton's copying of oriental cloisonné, where Japanese-inspired designs were used to decorate shapes based on archaic Chinese jades or bronzes, along with Neo-classical forms. Another style popular throughout the 19th century was Imari. The original came, of course, from Arita in Japan, but its success in Europe encouraged Chinese potters to add their version of Imari to the list of porcelains exported to the West. As a result English potters producing their own versions of Imari during the 19th century often did not know whether the models they were using came from China or Japan, or even 18th-century Europe. Professional collectors, museums and antique dealers were often little better, failing regularly to distinguish between original oriental ceramics and later copies. The emphasis in any case at this time was on the decorated ceramics of the Ming and later periods, wares prone particularly to later copying; the plainer, simpler wares of the Song and earlier periods were virtually unknown. Decoration was all-important, and so Chinese and Japanese ceramics had to fulfill the requirements of late 19th-century decorative design criteria. A direct result was that when English potters began to turn from Japanese to Chinese ceramics for their inspiration, they were quite likely to be using inadequate or inaccurate models. Furthermore, they may well have been inspired, not by original Chinese ceramics, but by later copies, or even by contemporary French interpretations of Chinese ceramics. It is therefore important, when considering Howson Taylor's orientalism, to try to identify exactly the types of Chinese ceramics he may have used as models. Even with the advantage of hindsight, it is easy to misinterpret what he could or could not have seen. It was not until the 1920s that connoisseurship in Chinese ceramics began to attain its present levels of expertise and it was equally not until the 1920s that collectors' tastes began to swing away from the decorative wares of Ming and later periods towards the so-called primitive ceramics of the Song, Han, Tang and earlier dynasties. In terms of style, Howson Taylor's pottery was virtually fully developed by the outbreak of the First World War, and what followed during the 1920s was, with the obvious exception of the crystalline glazes and the later shapes, a matter more of refinement than novelty. This point is important in any consideration of Howson Taylor's Chinese sources for it would be an easy mistake to assume that he had ready access to types of wares that at that time had little appeal to both public and private collectors.

There are three types of Chinese ceramic that seem to be relevant although, in the lack of any written evidence by Howson Taylor himself, their precise impact upon Ruskin Pottery has to remain largely conjectural. The first are the Jun wares, a type related to northern celadons and produced during the late Song and Yuan dynasties. Their characteristic feature is a thick opalescent ash glaze, normally an opaque sky blue with a light turquoise tinge caused by small quantities of iron oxide reacting during the reduction of firing, over a stoneware body. The quality of the glaze is often irregular, the result of accidents in the kiln, but this irregularity has always been considered a virtue, both by the potters themselves and by subsequent collectors. Shapes are rounded, elegant and deliberately exploit harmony and simplicity. From the 12th century, this irregularity was increased by the habit of splashing copper oxide over the glaze prior to firing, to create a contrast between the even blues and the uneven red tones created by the copper. At first the reds were limited to little more than delicate blushes, but they became increasingly prominent during the 13th century, turning into random areas of rich purple. Splashed Jun, as the style is known, is generally found on bowls, vases, boxes and tripod incense burners and its use was limited to the decoration of small-scale wares. The style is considered to have passed its peak by the 14th century, when the pottery became coarser and the decoration cruder and more garish in colour.

However, the remarkable delicacy, the simpler styles and the soft colours of the best Jun wares enjoyed a long-lasting popularity and encouraged potters in later periods to reproduce them. Ming potters made a version of Jun ware, but their shapes were generally more elaborate and they used more copper to create far stronger overall flambé effects during the reduction firing. Reproductions continued to be made during the Ming and Qing periods, and Jun ware is included in the list of replicas of antique wares being made at Jingdezhen published by Tang Ying, one of the supervisors of the site, in 1736. Reproductions were also made through the 19th century. It is hard to distinguish the best Jun copies from the originals, and so it is not necessary to know whether Howson Taylor saw real Jun ware or later reproductions. Much more important is the characteristic style of the Jun wares, regardless of their date, for the random copper splashes seem to have been one of a number of Chinese reduction fired glaze effects echoed by Ruskin Pottery, although more

typically in the soufflé glazes than in the flambés.

Also important are the links with the monochrome glazed wares produced by Ming dynasty potters from the late 14th century onwards. There were two main types of monochrome glaze used at this time, cobalt blue and copper red. The red was the harder to control in the kiln and so the colours range from brown to a true cherry red, with considerable tonal variation on each piece. The unpredictability of the colour may have contributed to the red wares becoming less common from the end of the 15th century, but prior to that date the technique had been fully developed to reach a peak during the Xuande period (1426-35). From the point of view of the Ruskin Pottery, the cobalt blue wares were just as important as the red wares and were, in any case, probably more accessible in the West, having been made consistently over a longer period. Some of the early Ming monochromes were additionally decorated with anhua, or secret, designs, patterns carved or incised into the body of the ware and then hidden by the glaze to be revealed when the finished piece was held up to the light, and this technique may also have influenced Howson Taylor. The simple stylised floral or foliate ornament incised or painted on early Ruskin pottery often has a similar quality of secretiveness, with the pattern deliberately hidden beneath the glaze. However, the Ruskin effects could equally well be as much the result of poor potting and firing as conscious copying of the anhua technique.

Other colours were introduced during the Ming period and some of these were also used in monochrome form, notably yellow, developed from antimony in the 15th century, and a range of greens and browns and an aubergine developed in the 16th century. Some of these were used overglaze and so do not relate directly to Ruskin but the high fired underglaze colours do seem to have been influential.

Even more important are the monochrome glazed wares produced during the Qing dynasty, and particularly during the Kangxi period at the start of the 18th century, for these relate directly to the glaze effects achieved by Howson Taylor. The restoration and reopening of the kilns at Jingdezhen after 1681 heralded a period of porcelain production in China unequalled in its dazzling diversity, its originality, its technical excellence and its kaleidoscope of multicolour and monochrome glaze and decorative effects. The techniques of the past were rediscovered and improved and, at the same time, new styles were developed, many of which reflected the impact upon Chinese potters of the newly opened western European markets. Especially notable is the restrained style associated with the Court, simple yet sophisticated and seen at its best in some of the monochrome glazed wares. Among these was the reduction fired copper red, and over the next 100 years it was developed to a level of excellence undreamt of by Ming potters. By mastering the complex reduction firing process the Qing potters were able both to produce reds of great evenness and regularity and to create multicoloured effects with the reds turning to greens in irregular spots or blotches. Although yellow was considered the most important of the monochrome colours, and reserved for Imperial use, copper red wares often also enjoyed Imperial status. All shades of red were achieved, from a pale pinkish grey to a rich cherry red. This, in its most brilliant and intense form, was known as langyao, or *sang de boeuf*. On a good example the colour of the glaze will develop over the body of the vessel, from a pale greyish green at the neck to a deep crimson brown at the foot, with all the graduating shades of red in between. The glaze is thick and apparently translucent, giving the colour an illusion of great depth, and the control has to be absolute, with the glaze stopping evenly above the foot. Glaze dribbles spreading onto the foot, and having to be cut or ground off after firing, were often a feature of later *sang de boeuf* glazed wares, particularly those produced in the 19th century. Later in the 18th century the red colour was sometimes splashed with an opaque grey blue glaze, which formed random areas of rich purple over the red during the reduction firing.

The other great copper red glaze of the Qing period is the more subdued and subtle peachbloom, equally varied in colour but with a softer, more velvet-like finish. The colour variation is often more delicate, with a pale greyish pink shading to darker tones, and the overall effect may be mottled, with patches of green breaking through the reds. The best peachbloom glazes were frequently used for the specific group of eight small, elegant vessels designed for the scholar's writing table, and comprising vases of different sizes and shapes, water coupes, a brush washer and a seal colour box. The sense of harmony achieved by the balance of shape and glaze was a vital element at the time, and one that has been pursued by European potters since the middle of the 19th century. Other reds of the Qing period include an even grey red, known as liver red, a pale grey red known as ashes of roses, and a whole range of speckled reds mixed with greens, blues and other colours. Although the copper reds were of primary importance during the Qing periods, many other monochrome colours were also developed. The blues ranged from a deep Ming-type tone, through mazarin to a delicate pale colour known often as *clair de lune*.

The blue glazes were used on the same shapes as the copper reds and the subtle colours often emphasise the fineness of the potting. Related to the blues but quite different in technique were the so-called powder blues, where the cobalt powder, instead of being mixed with the glaze and applied to the ware in the usual way was blown dry onto the porcelain body through a bamboo tube with gauze stretched over the end. After clear glazing and firing, the ware emerged from the kiln with a striking mottled effect, at its best looking like lapis lazuli. There was also a range of opaque glazes, including pink, lime green, yellow, turquoise, brown and coral red, notable for the strength and evenness of their colour over the surface of the ware. Lacking the mystery and variation of the copper red and blue ranges, these colours had less appeal to potters in the West.

There is no doubt that in the hands of the Qing potters the reduction fired glazes reached their high point of development. The various copper red and blue glaze effects have continued to be produced in China up to the present day, but few recent productions can match the quality of those made at the start of the 18th century. For Howson Taylor the Qing monochromes must have had particular importance, and their influence is clearly visible in his high fired glazes, in his soufflé glazes and, above all, in his shapes. The links between Ruskin Pottery and earlier periods of Chinese ceramics are more tenuous and generalised, but there is a specific association with the Qing copper red and blue wares that seem to go beyond simple stylistic parallels. However, it would be wrong to disregard the impact of the Jun and Ming wares, for these have in common with Qing porcelain the technique of reduction firing. It is above all Howson Taylor's pursuit of the elusive goal of controlled reduction of transmutation firing that puts him firmly into the Chinese camp, and distances him from European traditions of decorative chinoiseries. It also links him closely to other European potters who were pursuing the same goal through the second half of the 19th century, and it is the work of these potters that was probably a more direct source of inspiration. The development of high temperature reduction firing occurred later in Britain, and so British potters were able to follow a path that had been pioneered in France, Germany, Scandinavia and the United States. Howson Taylor was therefore able to benefit directly from two major sources, several centuries of Chinese expertise and over 50 years of European experimentation, and together these enabled him to master a technology hitherto little known in practical terms in Britain. It also enabled him to avoid the temptation of simply trying to reproduce Chinese reduction fired ceramics. He used Chinese shapes, because he thought they could not be bettered, he used Chinese glaze technology, or rather European interpretations of it, but he did not make European replicas of Chinese wares. To have done so would in any case have been pointless, for replicas produced in China were readily available throughout his lifetime. The Chinese influence upon Ruskin Pottery is therefore in some ways more philosophical than practical, for Howson Taylor's main aim was to conquer the reduction firing technique and in the process to push forward the boundaries of ceramic knowledge. To be able to reproduce Chinese glazes was merely the first step in a long process of experimentation and improvement that ultimately enabled Howson Taylor to create a range of reduction fired wares that were simply more varied, more exciting and more dramatic in their colour effects than anything that had been seen before. That he was able to do so was, in some ways, a direct reflection of the progress made by European late 19th-century potters along the road towards the mastery of reduction firing. Certainly the Chinese mastery during the Qing period was absolute, but it was a mastery whose secrets were firmly locked in the wares of the time, and no amount of studying of the finished ceramics would have made those secrets accessible in later centuries. Chinese technical manuals were used by French potters but they were only a starting point. In stylistic terms the Chinese influence upon Ruskin Pottery was therefore considerable, but for his technology Howson Taylor had to look to Europe, and above all to France.

European interest in Chinese red glazed ceramics did not really develop until the 18th century, when it was fired by a number of descriptions of the Imperial kilns at Jingdezhen brought back by French and English visitors. Few examples had in any case made their way to Europe before the 18th century, although one of the earliest may well have been a silver mounted red glazed Ming period bowl, presented to Queen Elizabeth I in 1572. The earliest known description by a European of the Jingdezhen kilns and the processes of Chinese ceramic manufacture by a European is contained in the two letters written in 1712 and 1722 by the Jesuit missionary Père d'Entrecolles. This well-known and much-quoted source was published in France in 1735 and in England the following year. D'Entrecolles witnessed all the processes of ceramic manufacture, including the preparation of the red glaze, but he was never able to discover the actual ingredients, how they were mixed, or the secrets of firing. However, he was able to report that the red came from copper:

'This red glaze is made from granulated red copper, and the powder of a certain stone or flint that is a little reddish in colour, pounded together in a mortar and mixed with a boy's urine and with the ordinary white glaze. I have not been able to learn the preparation of these ingredients, and those who know this secret are very careful not to divulge it.'

The second source to come to Europe was the six volume *T'ao-Shuo*, a description of Chinese ceramics largely written by a scholar called Chu Yen and published in 1774. In the third volume the writer discusses the copper red wares fully, but once again the precise ingredients and method are not revealed. The third source, and in some ways the most important, was another Chinese work, the *T'ao-Lu*, published in 1815. This contained very full descriptions of Chinese ceramics and Chinese manufacturing centres, including Jingdezhen, and included technical information about copper red glazes, among many other wares. This work was translated into French in 1856 by Stanislas Julien who incorporated much of it into his book *Histoire et fabrication de la porcelaine ouvrage traduit du Chinois*. A full English translation did not appear until 1951. Julien was also important because of his friendship with Jacques-Joseph Ebelmen, who became director of the French national porcelain manufactory at Sèvres in 1847, following the death of Alexandre Brongniart. It was at Sèvres that the first European attempts at making a Chinese copper red glaze took place. Fully supported as it was by the state, Sèvres was in some ways an official ceramic research centre, with both the time and the money to carry out costly and complex experiments. Brongniart, director from 1800 to 1847 had established well founded research traditions at Sèvres, and much of the experimental work carried out under his direction had been included in his famous book, *Traité des arts céramiques*, first published in 1844. In order to improve contemporary bodies and glazes, Brongniart encouraged his technical staff to analyse samples of historical pottery and porcelain brought to France from all over the world, and it was he who first suggested that French missionaries working in China should send back both Chinese ceramics and the raw materials used by Chinese potters. When he took over as director in 1847 Ebelmen continued this practice, and one of his first tasks was the analysis of various samples of Chinese porcelain, including fragments of red glazed wares, sent to Sèvres by Père Ly and Monsieur Itier. Armed with the results of the analysis, and with information gleaned from Julien's translation of the *T'ao-Lu*, the Sèvres chemist,

Alphonse-Louis Salvetat, set to work to reproduce the reduction fired copper red wares of China. Preserved in the Musée National de Ceramique at Sèvres are six copper glazed wares produced by Salvetat in 1848. Predominantly grey and smoky, with only occasional flashes of red, these apparently insignificant pieces represent nonetheless the first known successful examples of reduction fired copper red wares to be produced outside China by the high temperature transmutation process. In order to create these effects Salvetat had to use several firings, and it must have become clear at that time just how difficult and expensive the process could be. European potters began to understand the enormous scale of Chinese production, and the vital Imperial support that kept the Jingdezhen kilns going. For every successful red glazed pot produced during the Ming or Qing periods, there could have been hundreds of failures.

Salvetat continued his experiments, publishing more results in *Les Lecons de céramique* in 1857 and in his expanded edition of Brongniart's *Traité* issued in 1854. Descriptions of reduction fired red glazed wares began to appear in other books, for example J Marryat's *History of Pottery and Porcelain*, published in 1868 and P Burty's *Industrial Arts*, issued the following year, but no potter seemed prepared to follow Salvetat's lead for some years. Edouard Peyousson, working at Limoges, developed a range of high temperature colours from 1865, while Theodore Deck began to experiment with monochrome colours and glazes in the late 1860s. Equally important during this period was a broad interest in the history of Chinese ceramics, with a number of industrial potteries making copies or versions of Chinese wares. Notable among these was Minton, whose French art director Léon Arnoux successfully recreated Song and Jin style crackle glazes in 1862, a remarkably early date for the appreciation of the wares of those dynasties. During the 1860s and early 1870s Minton also produced a wide variety of Chinese-style monochrome wares, using strong green, yellow, turquoise, aubergine, red, brown and other glaze colours on classical Chinese vase shapes. However, these were lead based majolicas rather than high temperature glazes, and the emphasis was on the colour rather than the technique. Interest continued during the 1870s, encouraged first by the publication of A Jacquemart's *History of the Ceramic Art* in 1873, which contained a detailed description of the effects of chemical reactions on copper glazes during reduction firing, and second by the inclusion in 1877 of details of Salvetat's methods and experiments in a new edition of Brongniart's *Traité des arts céramiques*. At the same time, new museum displays of Chinese ceramics, such as that organised in 1876 by A W Franks for the Science and Art Department at Bethnal Green Museum, facilitated the detailed study of actual examples. However, it was not until 1880 that the next generation of European reduction fired copper glazed wares was produced, with several potters claiming success. Hermann August Seger, director of the Chemical-Technical Experiment Station at the Royal Porcelain Factory, Berlin, developed in 1880 a new soft paste porcelain which was used for the production of copper red wares, and his experiments over the next two or three years led him to claim to be the first European to master the Chinese process. He was able to produce considerable quantities of copper red wares to a standard of consistency previously unobtainable in the West. He published the results of his experiments and his recipes in 1883, concise and fully detailed records to substantiate his claims. Seger's work certainly represented a considerable advance on the achievements of Salvetat, but he was not alone.

In 1882 Theodore Deck produced a range of reduction fired copper red wares, ranging in tone from dark brown reds to cherry red *sang de boeuf*, the fruits of experiments in copper glazing that he had been conducting since 1880. In 1881, an Austrian chemist, A Buenzli, from Krummnussbaum near Vienna, had exhibited a range of copper red glazed wares at Leipzig trade fair. At the same time, developments were also going on at Sèvres. In 1876 the sculptor and designer Albert Ernest Carrier had taken over as director, and he had encouraged his technical staff to pursue their experiments in reduction firing. In 1880 a new porcelain body had been developed by Charles Lauth and Georges Vogt. Named *pâte nouvelle*, this proved to be an ideal vehicle for copper red glazes. Research at Sèvres was also greatly helped by a report received in 1882 from the French Consul at Han-Keou, Scherzer, who had been commissioned by the French Ministry of Public Instruction to find out all he could about the methods of porcelain manufacture in use at Jingdezhen. In effect, Scherzer mounted a military expedition and the presence of his armed guards encouraged the Chinese potters to reveal the secrets of the Imperial kilns. Information and samples collected were sent back to France, and what they revealed enabled Sèvres to produce a range of reduction fired copper red wares, a selection of which were put on public view at an exhibition at the Union Centrale des Arts Décoratifs in Paris in 1884. Seger, the German perfectionist, dismissed the pieces made by both Deck and the Sèvres factory as too accidental in their variation and thus not commercial, but his aim was probably a level of consistency that had eluded even the Chinese potters. The fact remains that by the mid-1880s reduction fired copper red wares in Chinese styles and colours were being produced successfully in some quantities in France, Berlin and Austria.

These early achievements had been predominantly technical with the major roles being played by ceramic chemists. With the technological bridgehead secure, the emphasis switched during the latter part of the 1880s and the early 1890s to the artistic side of pottery making. The key figure in the next stage of development was the pioneer studio potter Ernest Chaplet. Born in 1835, Chaplet was working at Sèvres before he was 20, gaining experience and on occasions assisting established artists such as Emile Lessore. However, far more important in the light of subsequent developments was his friendship with Felix Bracquemond, an engraver, painter, and designer, a leading figure in the Paris contemporary art world with particular interest in Japanese art, and the director of an art pottery studio at Auteuil owned by the Limoges potter Charles Haviland. The two first met in 1871 and in 1875 Chaplet joined Bracquemond at Auteuil. Initially Chaplet concentrated on the production of terracotta and stoneware with naturalistic and Japanese-inspired decoration, often in the Barbotine, or painted slip, technique. In 1882 Haviland gave up the Auteuil studio and opened a new one in the rue Blomet in Vaugirard under the direction of Chaplet. In the meantime Bracquemond had introduced Chaplet to Chinese copper red glazed wares, instilling in him the burning desire to master this complex process. In 1883 Haviland employed a ceramic chemist, Lebrun de Rabot, to work with Chaplet at Vaugirard and from 1884 they began to produce a range of individual stonewares with reduction fired copper red glazes. The same year Haviland was able to exhibit Chaplet's work at the Union Centrale, alongside the pieces produced at Sèvres. However, both Chaplet and Haviland knew that the real challenge was to succeed with porcelain, a far more demanding material fired at a much higher temperature than stoneware. Helped by de Rabot, Chaplet continued to experiment and on 30th March 1885 he was able to write: 'J'ai défourné ce matin, le truc est trouvé, nous aurons des rouges samedi prochain; l'enfumage a parfaitement réussi.' From this point on, working first at the rue Blomet and later at Choisy-le-Roi, Chaplet continued to produce a great variety of reduction fired copper glazed wares on both stoneware and porcelain bodies. His approach was entirely creative and his pots with their irregular shapes, thick glazes and startling colour effects were unlike anything produced at Sèvres or Berlin, where the aim had been technical perfection rather than artistic individuality. It was Chaplet's creative approach that attracted Gauguin to work with him in 1886. Chaplet worked above all as an artist, using clay and fire as his chosen media, and it was not unusual for him to fire his wares up to six times in his pursuit of virtuoso creative effects. At the same time, he was an excellent and highly professional technician, fully aware that he had to master his technique completely in order to achieve artistic individuality. In many ways Chaplet can be regarded as the first of the modern generation of studio potters and he was the first European potter to realise that it was not enough simply to reproduce Chinese red glazed wares. The effects he created were unlike anything ever seen in China and raised the ceramic art to new heights of excellence. Shortly before his death in 1909 Chaplet burned all his notes and documents, to ensure that nobody could copy his work, but well before that date many potters, in France and in other countries, had followed in his footsteps. These included Auguste Delaherche who took over the rue Blomet studio from 1887 to 1892, Jean Carriès and P H A Dalpayrat, but an equally important figure was Taxtile Doat, working at Sèvres and elsewhere during the 1890s, who developed an extraordinary range of high temperature and reduction fired abstract glaze effects, notable examples of which were shown to great acclaim at the Paris International Exhibition of 1900. During the same decade Valdemar Engelhardt was achieving equally exciting and unusual glaze effects at Copenhagen.

The late 1880s and 1890s became, therefore, a period of remarkable achievement at the boundaries of ceramic knowledge. The emphasis was on the Chinese reduction fired copper red wares but the mastery of this technology led the new generation of studio potters into other, equally exciting directions. Multicoloured glaze effects, crystalline and other semi-accidental glazes and unusual shapes were pursued relentlessly, both in Europe and in America, and potters experimented continuously with bodies, glazes, firing techniques and new minerals such as uranium. Pieces were regularly displayed at the major international exhibitions and so public awareness of these new achievements was considerable. Although all potters still kept their own processes a closely guarded secret, access to detailed technical information was readily available, through scientific and ceramic journals and through important books, such as Taxtile Doat's *Grand Feu Ceramics*, translated into English and published in the United States in 1905. At the same time, familiarity with Chinese ceramics was increased by the publication of books such as W G Gulland's *Chinese Porcelain*, issued in 1898, by Stephen Bushell's *Oriental Ceramic Art*, published in the United States in 1899, and by improved museum displays.

It was against this background of enormous technical and artistic achievement in Europe that William Howson Taylor developed his own interest in high temperature reduction fired glazing. It is not possible to establish with any degree of certainty which European potters particularly influenced him, but he cannot have been unaware of the advances being made in Europe. Books and articles were readily available and artistic studio pottery had, by the 1890s, achieved considerable international standing. In 1894, for example, *The Studio* published an article entitled 'The Renaissance of the Potter's Art in France', which discussed the work of Delaherche, Clement Massier, Bigot and Dammouse, with suitable illustrations. In effect a retrospective review of the display in the Exposition Universale at the Champ de Mars in Paris in 1889, this article described wares by Delaherche as 'a collection of vases, jugs, plates and bottles of quaint form, relying for their decoration almost entirely upon the beauty of the coloured glazes which covered them.' Similarly, wares by A Dammouse in the same exhibition were described as 'stoneware over which red and other glazes are employed.' Four years later a far more significant article in *The Studio* by Gabriel Mourey described and illustrated a wide range of work by Delaherche, with comments by the potter himself. Both the attitudes and styles of Delaherche seem particularly relevant to the Ruskin Pottery. Quoting Delaherche himself, the author writes:

'The art of pottery is a jealous art, demanding absolute fidelity. One must work, and seek and find unceasingly, and finding is most difficult of all, for one's discoveries must be made wittingly, with intention. It will not do to leave one's work to chance, as so many do. We are grappling with a blind power – fire; of all the elements perhaps the most powerful and the most formidable, and we have to subdue and master it, and not let it conquer us. To this object all the potters' efforts must tend ... almost always we meet with results unforeseen, surprising and very often most interesting; and this is our best school. It behoves us to make use of the unexpected, for each time the oven is heated there are fresh lessons to be learnt by the attentive observer. The danger lies in letting oneself be fascinated by these surprises, and thinking these will suffice in themselves ... to be satisfied with results obtained in this haphazard way is to bring this admirable art down to the lowest level.'

Equally revealing are Mourey's own attitudes, very much the attitudes of the period:

'For my own part I prefer pottery devoid of all line work and decorative ornament, relying for its richness and beauty on the charm of the vitrified material, on the various effects of the fusion on the enamels, and on the oxidations.'

He could have been describing the products of the Ruskin Pottery.

Also important from the British perspective were the two exhibitions of Chinese ceramics organised by the Burlington Fine Arts Club, and held in London in 1895 and 1896, the second of which concentrated on coloured monochromes. Among others, William and Joseph Burton are known to have been influenced by these exhibitions.

The changing nature of oriental studies is also reflected in the work of Howson Taylor. Both in documents issued by the factory in its early days and in reviews of exhibitions prior to 1910 there are many examples of parallels being drawn between Ruskin pottery and Chinese ceramics. A promotional pamphlet issued in 1905 states: '... the colour effects are almost unlimited, an expert stating that they are equal to those of the best period of the Chinese Myng Dynasty', while the anonymous reviewer of the Arts and Crafts Exhibition held at Leeds City Art Gallery in 1904 declared: 'Nowhere, aside from the old products of China and Japan, is the exhibit to be surpassed for elegance of form, refinement of colouring, or purity of glaze.' Today, such statements have to be taken at face value for remarkably few wares seem to have survived from this early period, and some of the colours listed in the same factory pamphlet quoted above, 'blues, greens, purples, clair-de-lune, pink, crushed strawberry, yellow, turquoise, and combinations of these colours, also others which are more difficult to reproduce, such as a special blue, robin's egg blue, sang-de-boeuf, peach bloom, lustres, crystallines, shagreen ...' are either rare or even unknown among collectors. Similarly, the number of shapes in the early catalogues drawn directly from Chinese ceramics are quite limited. There is a marked increase in Chinese forms by 1913, and indeed the Chinese influence seems to increase steadily from that date, underlining the developing awareness among both potters and collectors of the true nature of oriental pottery and porcelain. In 1910 the Burlington Fine Arts Club exhibition was devoted to

Song and Yuan wares, under the title *Early Chinese Pottery and Porcelain*. In his foreword to the catalogue C H Read wrote:

> 'For many years past a few isolated examples of somewhat rude and apparently early pieces of Chinese pottery have been found in the market ... During the last few years a fair number of such pieces have been brought to Europe and it has been found possible to group them into classes.'

Over the next few years classification of styles and periods improved by leaps and bounds, aided by exhibitions, by the publication of catalogues and books that heralded the arrival of a new generation of scholars, such as W B Honey and Bernard Rackham, and by the founding, in 1921, of the Oriental Ceramic Society. One of the first papers to be published in the journal of this new Society was J N Collie's monograph on the copper red glazes. The fundamental change of attitude among collectors and connoisseurs of Chinese ceramics can, in any case, be seen in any comparison between the books of the 1900s and those of the 1920s and 1930s. In 1902 W G Gulland wrote the following:

> 'The Ming pieces we shall find poor in quality, shape and colouring as compared with the Qing ... and perhaps in some ways the finest china belongs to the Yung-Cheng (Yong Zheng) period (1723-36).'

From the 1920s everything changed and Bernard Rackham, writing in 1935, was able to turn the history of taste on its head:

> 'The discoveries which astonished the world in the beginning of the 20th century brought about a revolution in the aims and ideas of collectors. In the wave of enthusiasm which greeted the masterpieces, newly revealed, of the classic ages of Chinese art (T'ang, Song and Ming) there was a danger that the real merits of later works would be forgotten or overlooked.'

This revolution had been supported by the publication of books such as A L Hetherington's *Early Ceramic Wares of China* (1922) and R L Hobson's *Wares of the Ming Dynasty* (1923). At the same time, it is necessary to remember the lasting popularity of W G Gulland whose pioneering *Chinese Porcelain* was in its fifth edition by 1928, despite the revolution in connoisseurship and taste that had taken place.

Interest in the earlier forms of Chinese ceramics was also increasing among potters. The early 1920s saw the first appearance of the rather crude interpretations of early Chinese wares by studio potters such as Bernard Leach, but more significant were the serious glaze experiments undertaken during the 1920s by potters such as Reginald Wells, William Staite Murray and Charles Vyse, brilliant technical potters and enthusiastic followers of the route pioneered by William Howson Taylor. Taylor's dependence upon the Far East was now established and it is not hard to find critical comments underlining this point. A typical example can be found in *The Studio*, June 1926, in an article well illustrated by some fine examples of high temperature flambé pottery made by Howson Taylor:

> 'The red glazes (obtained by the use of an oxide of copper fired to a heat of 1,400C) are of extraordinary richness and brilliance and rival in this respect the best Chinese Flambé.'

However, in order to appreciate these later developments, it is necessary to look in greater detail at 19th and early 20th century attitudes to the design and manufacture of artistic ceramics in Britain.

Chapter II
ART POTTERY IN BRITAIN

The late 19th century was a period of change for British potteries both artistic and industrial. The emphasis on revivalism that had characterised the first part of the century was replaced by an enthusiasm for more exotic styles and a greater degree of individualism in areas of design and decoration. Throughout the period potters looked to cultures and periods as far apart as ancient Egypt, pre-Columbian South America and the Middle East for their inspiration, but the dominant source of ideas was always the Far East. Once the frontiers of Japan had been reopened to the West by the American expedition of 1854, the cult of Japanism swept through Europe like a tidal wave. Japanese art and design, both past and present, was an important feature of the international exhibitions of the 1860s and by the 1870s even the most minor British potters had felt the impact of decorative Japanism. Characteristic Japanese techniques, cloisonné, lacquer, bronze and inlaid metalwork, ivory and decorative pattern-making and printing on paper and textiles were copied by potters great and small, affecting both the shape and the surface decoration of a wide range of ceramics, while traditional Japanese forms and style were freely adapted for the British market by designers such as Dr Christopher Dresser.

At the same time, China remained an equally important, if less revolutionary, source of ideas. Blue and white, blanc de chine, jade and bronze continued to inspire British potters, but more unusual was the new interest in the monochrome glazes of the 18th century. The dramatic high temperature glaze effects achieved by the Qing dynasty potters were being appreciated increasingly in Europe and a number of potters set out to reproduce these effects, without in any way simulating the complex technology evolved by the Chinese. Large manufacturers were, from the 1860s, increasingly willing to identify the designers of their wares in shape books and catalogues and the artists employed as decorators were given greater freedom in signing their work. These changes were in part brought about by the large number of French and other European-based artists now working in Britain who were accustomed to the higher standing enjoyed by designers and artists on the Continent. Pressures for change also came from outside the traditional boundaries of the ceramic industry with students from the national schools of design, and amateurs, wanting practical experience in the decoration of pottery and porcelain. This resulted directly in the setting up of industrial art pottery studios, sponsored by major manufacturers such as Minton and Doulton to encourage students, trained designers and amateurs, both male and female, to make a more individual contribution to the design and decoration of ceramics. Later, other companies also operated independent design and decorating studios, notably Copeland and Wedgwood, while valuable support for greater individualism was given by the various annual decorating competitions, such as those run by the retailers Howell and James.

However, the most positive reflection of the move towards individualism was the setting up of a number of small and independent art potteries. This trend started in London in the early 1870s and within 20 years had spread to practically every corner of Britain where pottery could be made. Some drew on local traditions and styles, using local materials and craft skills, while others set out to conquer new fields, but in each case a degree of practical industrial experience proved to be essential. These new art potters drew their inspiration from a wide range of sources, cultures and periods, but orientalism in all its forms was always important. A number explored the decorative effects achieved by the semi-accidental blending of colour glazes, while others concentrated more on the decorative aspects of Japanese design. Particularly significant was the widespread interest in red and yellow glazes, colours achieved both by the revival of historical techniques and by the experimental use of new minerals and oxides. An example of the former was William de Morgan whose fascination with Hispano-Moresque and Renaissance lustre effects has been well documented, while among the pioneers of the latter was the chemist William Burton who was involved in experimental glaze development for both Wedgwood and Pilkington from 1887. British potters in the late 19th century shared the common preoccupation with red glaze technology, but they had to go through several stages of development before they were able to achieve the goal of full reduction fired flambé colours. The difficulties involved in achieving, and maintaining, a good red glaze had been well known since the 18th century, with potters traditionally relying on iron as the basis for the glaze. By the 19th century most tones of red from a pale pink to a deep brown could be achieved by the use of calcined sulphate of iron, but other minerals were also used, including lead, cassius and gold. A consistent ruby red glaze was successfully produced by a number of companies, including Minton and Moore Brothers, and the colour was not uncommon by the 1870s. Although it was often used to decorate orientally inspired wares, it was in no way an oriental colour, being achieved through conventional, rather than reduction fired techniques, and even the richness of the red bore little resemblance to those based on copper. Among the many potteries which produced red glazed wares between the 1880s and early 1900s are Bretby, Burmantofts and Poole.

At the same time a number of potters in England were turning their attention to the old Renaissance technique of reduction firing in order to revive the strong lustre effects in copper and red tones associated with these wares. Much of the inspiration for this came from the publication in 1873 of C D E Fortnum's *Descriptive Catalogue of the Maiolica, Hispano-Moresque, Persian, Damascus, and Rhodian Wares in the South Kensington Museum*, a work that reflected current enthusiasms for both Renaissance and Middle Eastern ceramics. Reduction fired lustre plaques painted in historical styles by F W Moody for Minton and the range of ruby lustre vases and plaques made in the late 1880s by Maw and Company, some of which were designed by Walter Crane, are typical examples. However, more significant was the contribution made by William de Morgan. In 1872 an extensive correspondence started between de Morgan and various member of the Wedgwood family that was to continue for the next 30 years, and included in this was considerable discussion about lustre firing. De Morgan certainly received guidance from Wedgwood on firing techniques, and some of his earliest wares were fired at Etruria. When he had his own kiln, he maintained his experimental approach, and his mastery of the reduction fired lustre process can be judged from his wares. On 31st May 1892 he delivered a famous lecture on the subject of lustre decoration to the Society of Arts. Published in the Society's journal a month later, this detailed his researches in the field and gave both recipes and full description of the various ways he had used to achieve reduction fired copper and red lustre glaze effects. De Morgan used mainly the traditional process of applying copper compounds to the previously glazed surface of the ware, which was then fired at a relatively low temperature. He did not use the Chinese method whereby the copper was applied to the surface incorporated in a glaze or slip, and then reduction fired at a much higher temperature. British potters at this time tended to stick with these traditional low temperature methods, using reduction

firing largely as an historical technique, whereas their contemporaries in France were concentrating on the Chinese-style high temperature reduction fired flambés.

An equally traditional approach was used in the decoration of the lustre wares made by the Pilkington Tile and Pottery Company at Clifton Junction, near Manchester, from 1906 to 1928. The lustre glazes and the technique of reduction firing used to achieve them were developed by William Burton who had been appointed as technical and artistic director when the factory opened in 1898. Having worked previously as a chemist for Wedgwood, it is likely that Burton was familiar with De Morgan's work. The Pilkington lustre wares are highly coloured, but particularly notable are the strong reds. More interesting in the context of contemporary activities in France were Pilkington's earlier products, a range of wares decorated with experimental glaze effects developed by Burton. Dramatic colours, crystalline and opalescent effects and a conscious exploitation of the unpredictable nature of high temperature and reduction firing characterised this new pottery. The first of the new glazes was Sunstone, with its brown crystalline effects, developed by Burton's brother Joseph in 1893. This was followed by a green version. From about 1900 a range of other colour glazes was developed, including turquoise, purple, lavender, orange, ultramarine, dark green and red, many of which featured sparkling opalescent and crystalline effects. At the same time, Burton began to experiment with copper red glazes and reduction fired transmutation effects, having been excited both by Chinese examples, and by the flambé wares shown by contemporary French potters at the Paris Exhibition of 1900. Many of these effects were first shown at an exhibition of 'New Lancastrian Ware' held at the Graves Gallery, London in June 1904. Burton was among a number of British potters who particularly admired Theodore Deck, whose achievements had been closely followed in Britain since his first display of copper red glazes had been shown in Paris in 1880.

Another man who shared Burton's appreciation of Deck's work was Bernard Moore. Born into a well-established Staffordshire family, Moore, in partnership with his brother Samuel, took over the running of the family business, St Mary's Works, Longton, in 1870. Trading as Moore Brothers until the sale of the business in 1905, they developed a reputation as makers of high quality tableware and ornaments in bone china and earthenware, winning a gold medal at the Sydney International Exhibition in 1879. By training and inclination a technical potter and chemist, Bernard Moore began the experimental production of red glazes in about 1893. Initially, like de Morgan and Burton, he concentrated on the low temperature reds, using the same traditional process to produce both overall effects 'and painted patterns in red flambé, a technique well described by one of his paintresses, Hilda Carter:

> 'The Rouge Flambé was mixed into a grey slurry with a medium which I suspect contained ball clay, mixed to consistency which enabled the paintress to produce intricate designs, always visible during the decorating process against the white glazed background of the piece. The medium was not affected at the first firing except to deposit the Rouge Flambé which dried on as a grey deposit. This was finally polished off to reveal the typical red pattern.' (Aileen Dawson, *Bernard Moore, Master Potter 1850-1935*, Richard Dennis 1982, page 77)

Moore's experiments continued to the early 1900s but he seems to have used the knowledge gained, not to develop new ranges at his own factory, but to expand his activities as a consultant. Important was his association with Doulton, which started in 1901 at the suggestion of the company's art director, John Slater, who along with Charles J Noke, shared the common enthusiasm of the period for red glazes and flambé effects. Moore worked with Cuthbert Bailey, son of the factory manager C J Bailey, with the aim of producing a copper red flambé glaze that could be commercially consistent and economically viable. The fruits of this partnership were first put on public display at the St Louis Exhibition of 1904, and the critical acclaim they received was considerable. Eminent authorities compared the Doulton flambés 'with the best examples from the East' and suggested that they could 'rival the finest of the Chinese' while at the same time giving Bernard Moore much of the credit for the achievement. Doulton won 30 awards at the Exhibition, including two Grand Prix and four gold medals, and the judges again picked out the flambés for special mention. With the advantage of hindsight, it is easy to see that the Doulton flambés have actually little in common with Chinese copper red glazed wares. They were even in colour with a highly glazed surface that reflected the consistency and finish of industrial production, and they lacked the subtle irregularities of the Chinese wares. They were certainly a remarkable technical achievement, but they could not really be compared with either the Chinese flambé wares or the productions of the French studio potters. It is also likely that the technology used was far closer to the traditional methods of reduction firing used by de Morgan,

Burton and others than to the true oriental process of high temperature reduction copper glazing. Another company to win a Grand Prix at St Louis was the Ruskin Pottery, an award marking the first appearance of its wares on the international stage.

Following the financial débâcle that compelled Bernard Moore to sell St Mary's Works in 1905, he set up in business again on a much smaller scale, establishing a ceramic consultancy and a little art pottery in terraced premises in Wolfe Street, Stoke-on-Trent. Here, he pursued his experiments, concentrating now on recreating genuine Chinese copper red flambé glazes, along with a whole range of unusual glaze effects based on various metallic oxides. A small publicity brochure lists some of the specialised glaze effects in use at Wolfe Street: 'Sang de Boeuf, Peach Blow, Haricot, Rouge Flambé, Transmutation Glazes, Hispano Moresque, Gold Flambé and Collectors' Ware', and it is clear that with the help of his assistants and paintresses, Moore produced a wide range of art pottery from about 1907 to about 1930. His reputation was such that, on 23rd April 1913, King George V and Queen Mary included a visit to the Wolfe Street premises on their royal tour of the Potteries. While many of Moore's effects were achieved at low temperatures, there is no doubt that he was also able to master the process of high temperature reduction firing and produced wares that could stand beside their Chinese models. It is hard to establish when these were first made and for the majority it may have been as late as the 1920s, by which time other potters, William Moorcroft for example, had joined the list of those who had successfully reproduced the fugitive copper reds of the Chinese potters.

In comparison with the Ruskin Pottery, Bernard Moore's output was quite limited and yet at the same time he was the most revered among the English experimental potters of the early 20th century, partly because of the glowing reports of his abilities published by his friend William Burton. In 1902 Burton's book A *History and Description of English Porcelain* first appeared, with a fulsome description of Moore's work:

> 'Both French and German potters at length succeeded in producing effects in this manner, which, if not identical with the Chinese, were, at all events, worthy of comparison with them. Hardly anyone has known, however, that a Staffordshire potter – Mr Bernard Moore, of Longton – has been equally successful, and in addition to producing rich red and sang-de-boeuf glazes, has also produced novel and wonderful

effects by the use of metals other than copper, treated in the same way.'

Another Burton book, *Porcelain, a sketch of its nature, art and manufacture*, published in 1906, praises Moore's 'flambé and lustred porcelains', while also issued the same year was *Staffordshire Pots and Potters*, by F & G Rhead. These authors shared Burton's enthusiasm for Moore:

> 'In the Potteries today is one potter who has done something to redeem Staffordshire from the charge of indifference and decadence – Bernard Moore – a potter in the truest sense of the word. He is master of all the resources of the potter's craft, and his work alone shows Staffordshire still capable of coping with the potters of France.'

It is a sign of the times that, when these comments were written Moore was still producing predominantly low temperature flambés that could in no way be compared with contemporary French work, let alone with Chinese wares. The bulk of his high temperature work, which could have supported such praise, was still ahead of him. At the same time, neither author even mentioned William Howson Taylor, the one English potter working at that period whose wares could have stood comparison with high temperature reduction fired flambé glazed wares from France or China.

Chapter III
EDWARD RICHARD TAYLOR

In 1898 Edward Richard Taylor, the Head Master of the Birmingham Municipal School of Art, started a pottery business in association with his younger son, William Howson Taylor. Before taking this step, the Taylors had manufactured pottery in an experimental way at their home at 26 Highfield Road, Edgbaston. The success of this limited venture, which can be seen in some ways as a natural expansion of conventional School of Art practices, encouraged Edward Taylor to purchase some industrial premises, 173 and 174 Oldbury Road in West Smethwick, where he could start manufacturing on a commercial scale. In this three-storey building, at one time a malt house and formerly occupied by a wheelwright, sandwiched between the busy road and a waterway and the Great Western Railway's Stourbridge extension line, the Taylors set up in business as the Birmingham Tile and Pottery Works.

Edward Taylor's new venture, an ambitious and relatively expensive operation, was not undertaken lightly for he was able to draw upon his early experiences in the ceramic industry. Born in Hanley, Stoke-on-Trent on 16th June 1838, Edward Richard was the son of a local earthenware manufacturer, William Taylor. His mother, Ellen Howson, came from another local pottery family, her brother George founding in 1865 the substantial sanitary ware business that was to carry the Howson name into the second half of the 20th century. Following a local education, Edward went to work for his father, gaining the practical experience he was to use so constructively from 1898. At the age of sixteen he became a student at the new Burslem School of Art, joining the school on the day of its first opening in 1854 and remaining there until it closed some years later for lack of funds. The Master, W J Muckley, proved to be a very able teacher and Edward made great progress despite the somewhat primitive conditions offered by the school. A description, published in 1894 in *Edgbastonia*, a local Birmingham magazine, gives some idea of the difficulties under which the students laboured:

'This school ... stood in the back-yard of a public house, and underneath the one window a pig-sty had been erected, which was always fully occupied; with the practical result that the unfortunate students were either obliged to sit in a low room, half stifled with burnt gas, or else to suffer from a too close proximity to pigs if the window were flung open.'

When the school closed Edward, by now determined to become an art teacher, entered the National Training School for Art Masters at South Kensington, the forerunner of today's Royal College of Art. His progress was rapid and within three years he had gained the highest certificates granted by the Department of Science and Art. In January 1862 he was given the task of setting up a new School of Art in Lincoln, organising its administration and becoming, in the process, its first Head Master. Despite the small size of the premises and the rather basic facilities, the new school quickly flourished. The first students to sit the Science and Art Department examinations did unexpectedly well, the school gaining in the process the National Medallion for Elementary Design, and so it was soon moved to larger and more suitable premises. Edward Taylor had clearly found his vocation and under his guidance a number of students went on to win national awards and become artists of note, including Stanhope Forbes and Frank Bramley, later to be leading lights in the Newlyn School, William Logsdail, Markham Skipwith and J V Jelley. In 1878, the last year of Taylor's Head Mastership at Lincoln, the school won three gold medals, four silver medals, two bronze medals and 12 prizes in the national competition.

While still a student, Edward Taylor married in 1857 Mary Parr whose ancestor, Samuel Parr, was associated with the Chelsea Porcelain works in the 1740s. The couple had six children between 1858 and 1876, four daughters Elizabeth (Lizzie), Etty, Mary Ellen and Nelly Howson, and two sons, Edward John Bernard, born in 1873 and William Howson born in 1876. Despite the pressures and problems caused by the bringing up of this typically large Victorian family, Mary Taylor went on to enjoy a long life and did not die until 18th June 1935, a few days before her 98th birthday. Her longevity was inherited by her daughters Nelly and Elizabeth, but both sons were to die at the comparatively early age of 59. It was also during his time at Lincoln that Edward Taylor began to develop his considerable reputation as a painter. Specialising in portrait, landscape and genre scenes, Taylor exhibited regularly at the Royal Academy from 1865, showing over 30 works between that date and 1896. His subject matter and his lifestyle fitted well with the artistic taste of mid-Victorian Britain, and

Photograph of Edward Richard Taylor, Headmaster of the Birmingham Municipal School of Art, published in the July 1894 edition of 'Edgbastonia', a local monthly magazine.

his paintings were popular and sold well. Some were well received by critics, and reproduced in magazines such as *The Graphic*. The titles often tell all: *Her Wedding Ring* shows a very Victorian domestic drama unrolling in a pawn shop; *Nearing Home* is a life-size scene of three sailors staring from the port hole of a man-of-war, while *T'Was a Famous Victory*, exhibited in 1883, shows a Chelsea Pensioner in front of Turner's painting of the Battle of the Nile in the National Gallery, recounting the fight to two young sailors. As models for the sailors, Taylor used his two sons. Describing the former in *The Academy*, W M Rossetti wrote:

> 'Very solid, forcible, and entirely real, both in expression and lighting, and in other qualities – in fact, a careful and excellent production, neglecting nothing that pertains directly to its theme.'

Equally characteristic are titles such as *Our Treasure, Not Up to Sample, Away, Netting, All Together Lads, A June Morning* and *On The Lookout for her Boat*. Popular also were his landscapes, views of Lincolnshire, Suffolk, Worcestershire, Cheshire and Yorkshire, scenes that often included the sea, rivers or historic buildings. He also designed stained glass, and painted panels to be incorporated into pieces of furniture.

Successful and well regarded by collectors, Edward Taylor was a good all-rounder with an eye well tuned to contemporary taste and his position in the galaxy of Victorian art was well described in an article about him published in 1894:

> 'Mr Taylor is an artist of versatility and freshness. He does not repeat a past success until it becomes an annual failure. He turns from figures to landscape, and from landscape to the sea, and from the sea to portraits. He does not paint perpetual marble until it looks more and more like the "real article" nor does he turn out a pair of languishing lovers once a year to suit the tastes of the public and the market of the print-seller. The village church with sunset effect, which from constant repetition every twelve months becomes more and more like that abomination of desolation, an oleograph, he knows not, nor can he count by the score portraits of pompous provincial mayors, all gold chain and oily satisfaction, subscribed for by inartistic fellow-townsmen, and destined to deck local Town Halls, to the honour and glory of mayordom. But although he is by no means "one sided" in his expression of art, he gives us, perhaps,

his best in landscape work, which constantly shows high poetic feeling, combined with technical power.'

A member of the Royal Society of Artists, Taylor was able to blend together effectively his skills and experience as a painter with the practical needs of the art school, drawing on both to write a number of text books that became required reading among students. These include *Elementary Art Teaching, an Educational and Technical Guide for Teachers and Learners* and *Textbook on Drawing and Design for Beginners.* The former, published in 1890 by Chapman and Hall, reveals Edward's interest in ceramic design. Included are designs for pottery shapes and designs explaining correct proportion, along with pages of designs for surface decoration based on foliage and flower forms. Both the shapes and the decorative designs were to re-appear once the pottery had been established. The latter, published by Macmillan in 1893, considers methods of teaching other than those which were required under the Code of 1862 Regulations for art schools but which were more in harmony with Edward Taylor's own principles and methods of teaching. The article on Taylor published in 1894 in *Edgbastonia* commented:

> 'Combined Socialism and Individualism – an antagonistic combination in the opinion of many – perhaps best expresses what there is of system in his art-teaching. Socialistic in order to economize teaching power and to stimulate *esprit-de-corps*, but individualistic in the sense that the one thing to be most eagerly looked for, fostered, and well-directed in the student is that individualism with which each one of us is particularized, which, properly developed, adds the highest charm to a man's life work.'

In 1878 Edward Taylor left Lincoln to take up the post of Head Master to the Birmingham School of Art, receiving as a leaving present from staff and students a silver centrepiece and tea and coffee service. In the late 1980s the centrepiece, an elegant object in a restrained Neo-classical style, was still owned by descendants living in California. During his time at Lincoln he had built up a school from scratch that, at the time of his departure, had become one of the most successful and highly regarded of provincial schools of art. In Birmingham he faced an even greater challenge. The school, crammed into the top floor of the Midland Institute, was short of money, equipment and dedicated staff. There were plenty of students but they were inadequately taught, morale was at a low ebb, and the few awards and medals gained in the national competitions did Birmingham

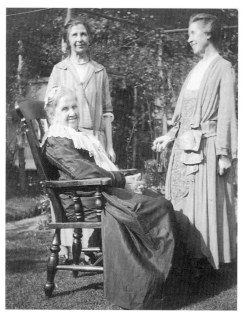

Edward Taylor's widow Mary, with her daughters Lizzie and Nelly, photographed during the 1920s.

Studio photograph of William Howson Taylor as a child, taken by Harold Baker of New Street, Birmingham.

little credit. Into this atmosphere Edward Taylor must have come like a breath of spring and his immediate impact upon both staff and students was memorable. Writing after his death, Kate Hall, a student and fellow teacher at Birmingham, tried to recall his arrival:

'Those who had the privilege of welcoming him will never forget his coming – his enthusiasm, his energy, and his marvellous power of inspiring all who came near him with his own spirit. He came in May, after the Government Examinations were over; by the end of June, when the School closed, he had won the affection and confidence of every teacher and student. When the School re-opened in September, nearly every important family in the town had a representative on the student list. Then started that happy and glorious relationship between Master and student which lasted all through the years, in spite of untold difficulties in the management of the School, caused by the fact that the students were so numerous and so eager, but the accommodation so limited and bad.'

Under Taylor's guidance the school expanded rapidly and the awards gained in national competitions improved year by year. Inadequate buildings were constantly enlarged and improved until at last a site was acquired and a new school erected. At the same time, in 1885, the new school came under the control of Birmingham Corporation, becoming the first Municipal School of Art in the country. Designed by Henry Chamberlain, the new school set

the standard for similar institutions all over Britain. Enlarged again in the early 1890s, the school, one of the largest in Britain, then contained 18 large class rooms and numerous offices and private rooms. Over the 20 years from 1880 to 1900 staff increased from 23 to 87. Fifteen branch schools were affiliated to it. In 1893 there were 3,111 students in a school of art that Edward Taylor had developed into 'an object of pride to all Birmingham men who understand of what great value a true taste for good art may be to the community.' Birmingham's success, and indeed Taylor's reputation, was based on the new teaching system he devised for the school. The basis of this was that 'design, composition, and invention should, in the interests both of pure art and of the artistic industries of the district, form as far as possible an essential of the work of every student, and should from the beginning go hand-in-hand with executive training.' A sense of design and the use of the imagination were seen from the outset to be as vital a part of art education as the teaching of technical and manipulative skills. This was a reversal of the traditional approach, and its success in the hands of Edward Taylor in some ways laid the foundation for the methods of art teaching that were to become commonplace in the 20th century.

At the same time, Taylor made great efforts to associate the school closely with local industries and to ensure that students were taught to appreciate the needs of the manufacturer, and to develop practical design skills that took into consideration the nature of the material, whether it be textile, wood, ceramic, metal or jewellery. Although it was often said at the time that Taylor was the first to teach crafts, he himself denied this, saying instead that his methods 'gave students an opportunity of producing their designs in the materials for which they were intended.' Certainly, familiarity with a variety of craft skills was an essential part of the curriculum, with classes teaching enamelling, mural-painting, stained-glass, wood carving, vase decoration and terracotta, as well as more conventional skills. At the same time, it is worth remembering that neither Birmingham, nor any art school in Britain, had a practical pottery making department. The first was not opened until 1901, at South Kensington. Birmingham played a leading role in bringing down the boundaries between the fine and the applied arts and of the best-known students of this period, W Langley, J W Wainwright, E S Harper, A J Gaskin, C Gere, F Mason, W J Payne, F Davis, S P Meteyard and others, went on to develop reputations in a variety of media. A history of the Birmingham School during the Taylor period is contained within *Made in Birmingham: Design and Industry 1889-1989*, published by the Design History Society.

Above all, Taylor seems to have been an inspired teacher, taking care to devote time to even the most unpromising of his students. To quote Kate Hall again:

> 'Undoubtedly, one secret of Mr Taylor's success was the result of his method of always looking first for "the good" in a pupil's work; then, when he had given a word of encouragement, the pointing out of the faults did not depress the worker. He had a wonderful way of making everyone feel the possibility of doing *something*. He had the power of drawing out whatever natural gifts his pupils might possess, and inspired an artistic spirit and an appreciation of the beautiful ... He was a great teacher, a wise counsellor and a true friend.'

The popular esteem enjoyed by Taylor was underlined both by his harmonious relationship with his management committee and the City Council, and by the number of presentations he received. The first, an illuminated scroll accompanied by a series of paintings, a bookcase, secretaire and armchair, along with a number of books including an illustrated Shakespeare, was made to him by staff and students in 1885, at the time of the school being taken over by the Corporation, but far more elaborate were the celebrations that surrounded his retirement, in June 1903. The occasion was fully described by Kate Hall, his most devoted follower:

> 'Mr Taylor retired in 1904 (sic). As the time drew near when we knew we must say "good-bye" to our chief – (for by the law of the Corporation everyone has to leave when Father Time points to 65 years passed) – we wondered how we could best express our love, appreciation and gratitude. He left us at the close of the School Session at the end of June, 1904 (sic). Certainly such a demonstration will never take place again. *He* was the "Father of the School". Old students, with present students and the staff, all vied with each other as to who should do the most. Committees were held, and it was decided that all the gifts presented should be the work of the students and executed in the School. Then, of course, everyone wanted to add his or her portion. May I name a few? An address beautifully illuminated and printed, bound in embossed leather; on the front side his monogram in enamel, on the under side this inscription: – "Magistro nostro perenni. Perennis et laus, et gloria." Six silver teaspoons in a case, each spoon the work of a lady. A volume of illustrations from the students of the Book Illustrating Class, bound in the Book-binding Room. A case embroidered to contain "the cheque". A silver stamp-box; a paper-knife, a match-box, two enamels, one from his latest gold medallist; etc. The Office Staff presented a writing-case, and the Industrial Staff an umbrella. The School looked like Fairy-land, decorated with lovely flowers in every part. Students from far and near crowded the rooms. The entrance was illuminated when evening shadows fell, and when the hour of departure struck, carriages were at the door to convey the Chief and his family and his gifts, to his home in Edgbaston. These were followed by bikes and motor cars.'
> (Kate A Hall, *A Notable Art Master: An Appreciation*, Edgbaston, Birmingham, December 1913).

An even more detailed report was published in the *Birmingham Daily Post* on 29th June 1903.

It was probably the practical application of his own teaching principles that enabled Edward Taylor to develop a new interest in ceramics. His early experience of work in the Potteries provided a foundation upon which he was able to build a new enthusiasm for the design and manufacture of art pottery. It is likely that the interest that led him to start making pottery at his home was first developed in the class room. He shared his enthusiasm with his son William who, with his brother Edward, was a pupil of Five Ways Boys School, Edgbaston, a branch school of King Edward Grammar School, Birmingham. Both boys continued their studies by going on to the Municipal School of Art, joining the Science and Art Department. E J B Taylor, three years older than his brother, won prizes in most of the years that he was there and obtained his Art Masters certificate in 1894. William Howson Taylor is mentioned only once in the Annual Report of King Edward School and that is in 1895 (year to 31st December 1895) where, as a former pupil of Five Ways Boys School, he had obtained the following prizes during the year:

> Free Studentship
> First Class in freehand and perspective
> Second class in modelling.

However, unlike his brother who got a first class in life drawing in 1896 and a National Book Prize in 1897, there is no record of further prizes awarded to William Howson. He may have given up his art studies to become more involved in pottery, but there were no prizes for pottery. In 1897 he went to Stoke-on-Trent to spend some time learning practical pottery skills at his cousin's sanitaryware factory, Howson's Eastwood Works, situated near Hanley, beside the Caldon Canal. However, Howson's can have been of little help to William in developing his consuming interest in glazing. For this, he must have relied almost certainly on his father's library. It is clear that Edward Taylor's interest was more than simply artistic, for by the terms of his will his son William was allowed to select up to 30 volumes from his father's collection of books on ceramics, art and science. His library must therefore have been considerable and may well have contained the major 19th-century technical and artistic treatises by authors such as Julien, Brongniart, Salvetat, Gulland and others. Unfortunately there is no record of what the library contained, or what happened to it after Taylor's death. Equally unknown is the content of his son's library. Were it possible to establish which 30 books William Howson Taylor selected, writing the history of the Ruskin Pottery might be a simpler matter.

However, it is safe to assume that Edward Taylor had an enthusiasm for ceramics that was both practical and artistic, and it was this that led him to set up an experimental pottery workshop in his house in Highfield Road, Edgbaston at some point in the mid-1890s. Again, little is known of this workshop and how it was equipped, or what Taylor and his son produced. However, the existence of the experimental kiln in the garden is well documented. In any event, the experience gained was sufficient to encourage Edward Taylor and his son to set up in business as commercial potters, and they remained partners in the venture that ultimately came to be known as the Ruskin Pottery until Edward Taylor's death on 14th January 1912. His death, at the age of 73, followed some months of illness but until his health failed in June 1911 he had been deeply involved in the running of the pottery. An obituary published in the *Pottery Gazette* in February 1912 referred to Edward Taylor as 'the eminent art instructor, talented artist and artistic potter' and then went on to describe him as 'the initiator of the special production of artistic pottery which has been so successfully developed by his son, Mr W Howson Taylor, under the name of "Ruskin Pottery".'

Chapter IV
THE EARLY HISTORY OF THE RUSKIN POTTERY

It is hard to establish with certainty the early history of the Ruskin Pottery. Documentary evidence is meagre and most that does survive comes from indirect sources. Family papers seem to be virtually non-existent and so most historians have to depend on reported opinion and personal reminiscence, the latter often far removed from its source. Particularly hard to establish is the role played by Edward Taylor in the setting up and running of the business. Traditionally he has been given a minor role in both creative and technical terms, and has often been dismissed as the supplier of finance, but little else: a vague but benevolent figure happy to support the creative endeavours of his son.

The actual situation may well be rather different, and it is possible to argue that Edward Taylor was, until his death, if not the dominant then at least an equal partner in a venture that was dependent upon his creative and technical skills. That he was also the financial backer of a business that was, in economic terms, precarious, is without question.

During his lifetime William Howson Taylor, and other members of his family, referred to large sums of money being invested in the business by Edward Taylor. Evidence suggests that at least £10,000 of Edward Taylor's personal money was poured into the pottery during its early years, a sum probably equivalent in present day values to half a million pounds. The first question raised by this is the source of so relatively large a sum of money. Until his retirement Edward Taylor was fully employed as an art master. Even in his senior position at Birmingham Municipal School of Art he would not have earned more than a few hundred pounds a year. In addition he had the income from his books, and the fairly substantial sums he may have made as a successful genre, landscape and portrait painter with a secure reputation backed by regular appearances at the Royal Academy. However, it is unlikely that these various sources of income could have produced the £10,000 required. His wife, Mary does not appear to have been particularly wealthy in her own right, and she seems to have been wholly dependent upon him, along with her four daughters, three of whom never married, and her two sons. The elder son, Edward was becoming established in his own career by 1898, the year the pottery was founded, but William Howson was at that point still only 22. However, there is evidence of some degree of family wealth. First, Edward Taylor

married and his eldest daughters were born before he went to work at Lincoln, and during the early years of his marriage he was a student at South Kensington, with no obvious means of support. Yet, the family appears to have enjoyed a comfortable standard of living. Second, Edward Taylor stopped exhibiting at the Royal Academy in 1896 shortly after the death of his mother. Could a legacy from her have made it no longer necessary for him to sell his paintings, and made it possible for him to finance the pottery experiments at Highfield Road?

The second question relates to how the money was spent for it seems to be fairly certain that the whole of the initial investment had been swallowed by the pottery during the first few years of its existence. There are reports of a family meeting to discuss the future of the pottery and whether Edward should continue to support it in the light of the considerable expenditure to date. The outcome seems to have been a unanimous agreement that he should do so. The actual costs of setting up the pottery cannot have been that great. These included the purchase of the premises at Oldbury Road, the building of kilns and other pottery structures and the mechanical equipment required, along with supplies of coal, clay, glazes and so on. Bearing in mind the scale of the operation, this is not likely to have cost much more than £1,000. It is unfortunate that no accurate information has survived, but a parallel can be drawn with another pottery of the same period which is well documented. In 1913 William Moorcroft built and equipped a pottery from scratch for a little over £2,000. This was a much larger building, specially designed to house an already established business that employed 34 people with an estimated annual turnover of £7,000. Fifteen years earlier the necessary investment to establish a far smaller pottery in existing buildings in Oldbury Road must have been much less. There was also the question of wages, but with a maximum of nine employees during the early years the wage bill can never have been more than £500 per annum. It is therefore quite hard to understand where the money went. Even supporting continual glaze experiments cannot have been that expensive. William Howson Taylor, in an interview published in the *Birmingham Gazette*, on 21st December 1934 said that for over three years he worked and experimented at a cost of over £10,000 before he allowed a single pot to leave the factory, but

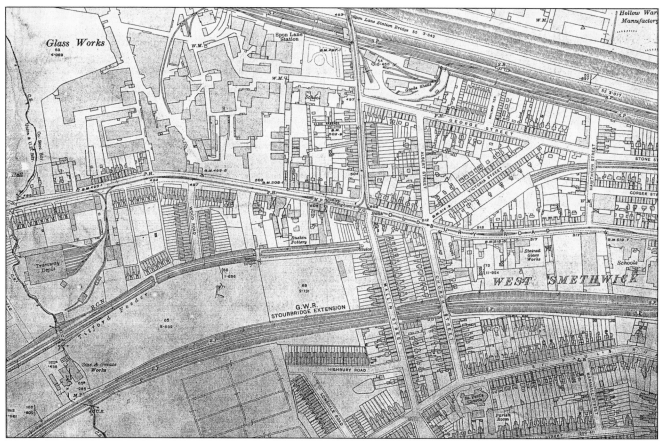

Above: The Ruskin Pottery, Oldbury Road, West Smethwick, *photographed at the time of its closure.*
Below: *Section from the 1919 Ordnance Survey Map of West Smethwick, showing Oldbury Road. The Ruskin Pottery occupied the plot of land to the immediate left of that marked on this map.*

the sums just do not add up, even if he was then talking in the values of the early 1930s. It is also recorded that Edward Taylor withdrew his initial investment from the pottery business or had been repaid in full before his death. Until that point he and his son had effectively been joint owners and partners, but from then on William Howson described himself as sole owner, with the family having no claim on the business from this point. That this large sum of money was able to be withdrawn without prejudicing the stability of the pottery raises several more questions, suggesting as it does that the business had, since about 1905, become remarkably successful. Yet, any study of the Ruskin Pottery as a business, that is to say a consideration of the relationship between the size and costs of the workforce and raw materials, the likely output of saleable pottery and the recorded sale prices of the finished goods, makes it clear that profits on the scale of at least £1,000 per year were simply impossible. In its first year of trading the Moorcroft pottery recorded a profit of £49. Unfortunately, it seems that the business details of the Ruskin Pottery have to remain a mystery.

At his death Edward Taylor's estate was valued at £11,920 after duty had been paid, and in his will he described himself as an 'artist'. Naturally, the Taylors, father and son, may have received monies from other, unrecorded sources. There may have been considerable property holdings, although these are not mentioned in their wills, and there may also have been shareholdings in other businesses. A possible candidate was the other family business, the sanitaryware factory founded by George Howson in 1865. On George's death in 1892 the business was transferred to his three sons, James Taylor, Bernard and Richard George, and in 1897 it became a limited company with the three sons holding the bulk of the shares. In the company's articles there were strict rules about the transfer of shares within the family, favouring close relations, and so there seems little chance of either Edward Taylor or his son having ever been major shareholders. Howson's remained a family business until 1966 when it was acquired by Shanks & Company, and became part of the Armitage Shanks Group. It was finally dissolved in 1985. The only ceramic links between the two branches of the family seem to have been, first, the time that Howson Taylor spent at the Hanley factory as a young man and, second, the short period of experimental production of flambé glazed wares undertaken from about 1912 by Richard Howson with the help of Edward Wilkes, a former employee of Bernard Moore. Howson Taylor's views of these wares are not recorded, but they cannot have aroused great enthusi-asm. The most obvious source of Taylor family wealth could have been Edward's father. William Taylor is known to have been an earthenware manufacturer in the Potteries, but the surviving rate books have no record of any pottery owned by him. However, a William Taylor was a partner in a number of companies from the 1820s, some of which were of substantial size. From records of other factories of this period, it is possible to deduce that William Taylor could have been a wealthy man without ever having his own pottery. As the younger son, Edward may not have benefited directly from his father's wealth until the death of his mother in 1896, but even in his early life there appeared to be plenty of family money.

In financial terms, the mystery continued after Edward Taylor's death, his son continuing to run a pottery that, despite an increasing reputation at home and abroad, can rarely have been highly profitable as a business. Yet, despite increasing costs, a well-paid labour force and a limited range of wares, some of which were expensive to produce and often highly priced in the market, the Ruskin Pottery remained in business, apparently trading adequately, for over 35 years. At his death in 1935 Howson Taylor's estate was valued at £10,916, duty paid, again a considerable sum considering the decline in sales that had followed the financial collapse of 1929. He had continued to look after his mother and his unmarried sisters, all of whom lived to great ages, his mother only predeceasing him by a few months, and while the family lifestyle was not extravagant, it was certainly comfortable. With the lack of evidence to the contrary, it is hard to avoid the conclusion that the Taylors were a wealthy family, and that the Ruskin Pottery was a private indulgence operated for their own purposes, with the primary concern being the quality of the wares rather than the profitability of the business.

It is not possible to establish what was produced by the pottery established by the Taylors at their house in Highfield Road, or if anything that they made was sold commercially. Certainly, nothing seems to be known that can be positively linked to that period, and records of the kilns suggest that output must have been very limited and largely experimental. Their activities became clearer with the setting up of the Birmingham Tile and Pottery Works, the official name of the business at 173 Oldbury Road. Trade directories of the 1899 to 1901 period record the company as a tile manufacturer, listing the business under the names of Taylor Brothers or Edward R Taylor. The listing of W Howson Taylor, earthenware manufacturer, at the Oldbury Road address does not appear for at least another year, but then continues unchanged in each annual directory until 1933.

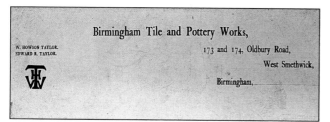

Letterhead of the Birmingham Tile and Pottery Works, c.1901.

There are no entries, domestic or commercial, for Taylor in 1934, and the Oldbury Road premises does not reappear in the directory until 1937, then under the name of C H White, wholesale chemists. The letterhead of the Birmingham Tile and Pottery Works shows W Howson Taylor and Edward R Taylor as partners, and also carries the WHT monogram that is found impressed on some pots of this early period. The official structure of the partnership appears to have remained unchanged until Edward Taylor's death. A trade mark application dated 2nd November 1909, for example, refers to 'Mr William Howson Taylor and Mr Edward Richard Taylor trading as W Howson Taylor' and other documents carry a similar style. W Howson Taylor was in use as a business name at least by 1901 and appears on printed documents of that period, and this may have led some authorities to believe that it was William who was the dominant partner from the beginning. In fact, the opposite may well have been the case. Edward appears to have been the driving force behind the business. The few letters that survive suggest it was he who handled the correspondence, and he who promoted the pottery and its products. In the past he has been dismissed as a self-publicist, ready to exploit his son's achieve-ments in his own name, but this really makes no sense. Edward Taylor was then a well-known and well-respected figure, and so he was ideally placed to draw attention to his new venture, despite the demands made on his time by the school of art. It is noticeable that, after his retirement in 1903, he was able to devote himself far more fully to the pottery.

It is not, of course, possible to establish with any certainty the exact division of roles between father and son, but it would seem reasonable to suggest that Edward Taylor may have been responsible for organis-ing and promoting the business and for designing the shapes and decoration, while William Howson Taylor ran the factory on a day to day basis at least until 1903 and developed the range of coloured glazes, drawing for the latter on his father's art school experi-ence and his father's library. In the event, such a division of labour is probably too clear cut, for the two men worked closely together to get the pottery going, sharing the enthusiasm and the responsibility.

However, much of the initial drive and impetus came from Edward Taylor, along with the money that kept the pottery in business and the promotional efforts that made it well known internationally after 1904. It has been suggested that the relationship between father and son was not particularly harmonious but there is no evidence to support this view. All the documents suggest a close working partnership and a well-knit family. It is also important to remember that, along with the 30 books from his library, Edward Taylor also left his son his large self-portrait. Often depicted as a rather dominant figure, Edward Taylor actually seems to have done his best to push his son to the fore. On printed documents William Howson's name always precedes that of his father and by using from the very early days W Howson Taylor as a trading name Edward seems to have tried to ensure that his son could take the credit. It is not known exactly why Edward withdrew his investment from the business but it does not seem that this act was in any way designed to prejudice the company's future. Clearly, by this time William Howson had sufficient funds to keep the pottery going from his own resources. Certainly William Howson seems always to have been aware of his debt to his father, and waited a year after his father's death before registering the business in his own name. Also, the collection of pottery given to Birmingham Museum in 1926 by William Howson Taylor was 'in memory of his father'.

In the course of his researches for his small monograph on the Ruskin Pottery, the first edition of which was published in 1975 by the Metropolitan Borough of Sandwell, James Ruston was able to interview at least six surviving former employees of the Taylors. The general impression seems to have been that working at Oldbury Road was a 'home from home' with both the Taylors taking care to remain on friendly terms with their workforce in what was an unusually intimate family business. Edward Taylor seems to have been the more outgoing of the two and has been described as 'a typical artist in appearance and temperament.' A kindly father-figure, fondly remembered riding his tricycle between Highfield Road and the pottery, Edward included in his will a bequest of £10 free of duty to every employee who had been at the pottery for over a year. William Howson Taylor was more withdrawn, but was always a generous employer, never unfriendly or unhelpful towards his staff, and both father and son were considered to be gentlemen in the traditional meaning of the word. There was no hint in these interviews of any areas of stress or disagreement between them.

Photograph of William Howson Taylor, taken in about 1913, and published in the March 1923 edition of 'The World's Work' to accompany an article about Taylor in the series 'Men and Women of Today'.

During the course of its existence, at least 25 men and women were employed by the Taylors at the Ruskin Pottery, with a maximum of 16 working there in the early 1920s, the factory's most expansive period. The first employees started work in December 1898, presumably having been recruited by Edward Taylor who also paid their wages, and so some production must have started in 1899. These facts do not tally with William Howson's 1934 claim that he experimented for three years before a pot was allowed to leave the factory, but such inconsistencies are unfortunately not uncommon in the history of the Ruskin Pottery. First to join was Florence Tilley, a local girl, and she was quickly followed by William Forrester, a turner and thrower formerly with Wedgwood, and his wife, Sarah Ann; Ernest Porter, a placer and firer; Emily Boswell, a paintress, and possibly Mrs Alice Wright, a sprayer. In broad terms these were experienced and well-trained personnel essential for the production of commercial ranges of pottery, and they were paid at rates equivalent to or above the going rates in the industry at the time. In later years, former staff of the pottery remembered the Taylors as considerate and benevolent employers who took care to protect their workers' interests. From the early 1900s advertisements, catalogues and critical reports in trade and art magazines all stress the point that all the glazes and colours used in the pottery were lead-free, and so the Taylors were well in advance of both much of the ceramic trade and the government legislation in this area.

With its premises fully equipped and its workforce assembled, the Birmingham Tile and Pottery Works was in business. However, even with the advantage of hindsight, it is hard to establish exactly what was produced during this early period. Very little seems to have survived from this time, despite a considerable output over the first four years, and positive attribution is often made harder today by the lack of marks and dating on the pieces themselves. In this period it is necessary to rely on the evidence of documents and reports rather than on the pottery itself, and luckily there are enough of the former to piece the story together.

To judge from their chosen company name, the Taylors must have made tiles. For the first three years of its existence the pottery was listed only in the brick and tile section of the local trade directory, and it is possible that tile manufacture, a fairly straightforward business given the right machinery and production expertise, was the mainstay of the pottery's output. Perhaps the Taylors made tiles to keep the factory fully employed and to subsidise other, more experimental areas of production. Certainly the tile industry at that time was still very successful, with many recorded manufacturers in Staffordshire, the Black Country, the Severn valley and other centres of production, and so the Taylors could well have decided to benefit from the continuing demand for tiles for both architectural and decorative purposes. The difficulty is simply that very few Taylor-made tiles are known today. Those that do survive reveal that the pottery was equipped with tile presses. Made from pressed powdered clay in the usual manner, the tiles are of conventional size and thickness, and have the standard back with ridged horizontal bars and the impressed name TAYLOR. The faces are glazed in blues and greens, occasionally with a hint of pattern under the glaze. Presses were also used for the production of other items, such as the architectural fittings, roundels and buttons, the last two later becoming in their turn significant sectors of the factory's production range. The few tiles that are known today are completely unrepresentative of at least three years' production, and so the assumption has to be made that Taylor tiles were either unmarked, and therefore remain unrecognised, or were relatively simple, and therefore indistinguishable from those of their many competitors. Unfortunately, there are no documentary clues as to the nature and scale of tile production at the Taylor pottery, but it must have been important as there was no other way at the time for the factory to have made any money. It is also possible that the Taylors simply manufactured blank, unmarked and undecorated tiles on a sub-contracting basis for other companies.

At the same time, hollow ware was clearly in production. From its earliest days the factory had a thrower and turner, and this area of manufacture was greatly expanded in 1901 with the arrival of William Nixon, a turner of great expertise who had also been trained at Wedgwood. Another employee to join at this time was Jack Cooksey, the packer and general handyman. Initially the factory relied on local clay supplies, a coarse brown marl from the Blakeley Hall Colliery in nearby Oldbury. Popularly known as 'tocky' this clay was refined in the factory to produce an adequate modelling body, and its distinct characteristics can be a help in the dating of early unmarked wares. The most common glaze of this period was chrome number 11. Based on chrome oxide, this produced a range of rich holly greens intermingled with blue on the brown earthenware body. The glaze was used to decorate a tea service supplied to the Duchess of Sutherland in 1900.

Other early glazes include a rose green, a celadon and an oatmeal. The first clear, documentary evidence of the pottery's history is its first catalogue, a

SOUFFLÉ GLAZES 1898-1914

A group of wares representing the early years of the Birmingham Tile and Pottery Company. Above left: a range of 6 inch (15 cm) tiles with mottled soufflé glazes, with raised moulded TAYLOR WEST SMETHWICK mark, and a clock face with an apple green soufflé glaze; above right: a range of moulded architectural fittings with blue, green and oatmeal soufflé glazes, including an electric bell push, a ceiling rose, door knobs and finger plates, all c1900 and unmarked; below left: vase (shape 6 from 'Forms in Pottery') with a brown 'tocky' body splashed with oatmeal glaze, 24 cms, painted mark Ruskin 1899 E136; below right: vase (shape 8 from 'Forms in Pottery') with 'tocky' body and moss green soufflé glaze overpainted with stylised flowers in turquoise, 15.2 cm, painted mark Taylor 189(9?).

Also purchased by the Victoria & Albert Museum was a patent inkwell, similar to those shown here (shape 19). Left, with liver pink and celadon soufflé glaze, dated 1909, right with dark blue soufflé glaze, both impressed PATENT and Ruskin marks, larger 8.5 cm diameter.

Wares purchased in 1901 from the Birmingham Tile and Pottery Company by the Victoria & Albert Museum, London. Above left: vase in 'tocky' body with streaked soufflé glaze, 22 cm, impressed TAYLOR; below left: vase with holly green streaked soufflé glaze, 20 cm, scissor mark; above right: bowl (shape 38) with orange soufflé glaze and painted band of vines, 20.3 cm diameter, impressed TAYLOR; centre right: tablewares in brown, blue and apple green soufflé glazes, plate 21 cm diameter. (Trustees of the Victoria & Albert Museum)

AGENT :—

G. T. BAGGULEY,

Stationer, Newcastle.

RUSKIN POTTERY.

W. HOWSON TAYLOR, WEST SMETHWICK, ENGLAND.

André & Sleigh, Ltd., Bushey.

André & Sleigh, Ltd., Bushey.

RUSKIN POTTERY.

W. HOWSON TAYLOR, WEST SMETHWICK, ENGLAND.

The colour plates included in the 1905 Ruskin catalogue, showing a range of soufflé, lustre and flambé glaze effects, along with painted foliate decoration and metal mounts.

Above left: cups and saucers and a plate in the 'tocky' body, c1900, with blue-green and apple green soufflé glazes and foliate decoration, the plate 17.7 cm and with impressed WHT monogram and painted scissor mark; above right: water jug (shape 86) with a mottled turquoise soufflé glaze, 22.8 cm, impressed oval mark and date 1906; below: group of wares with blue-green soufflé glazes, all with oval marks and dated 1906, left to right, vase (shape 246) vase (shape 307), scent bottle with silver stopper (shape 154) and a bowl. Tallest vase 22.8 cm.

A group of wares featuring painted underglaze foliate decoration. Above left: two beaker vases with mottled blue and ivory soufflé glazes, painted scissor marks, 30 cm; above right: a plate and a honey jar (shape 140) in mottled blue soufflé glazes, the jar with painted scissors mark, 11 cm; below: plate, covered vase (shape 79) and silver-mounted bowl in white and mottled blue soufflé glazes, the plate with a painted scissors mark, the vase dated 1905 and the bowl with a silver mark for 1908, vase 16.5 cm.

Large vase with overlaid soufflé glazes in tones of blue, impressed WHT monogram and painted A27, 43 cm.

Above: three vases with soufflé glazes, all with oval marks and dated 1905, left to right, mottled blue black toning to purple (shape 198), semi-matt apple green (shape 27), orange-red with green speckling, largest 27cm; below: vase (shape 200) with streaked dark blue soufflé glaze, oval mark and dated 1905, vase (shape 281) with mottled pink soufflé glaze, oval mark and dated 1906, 18 cm.

Above left: caddy (shape 362) with mottled blue soufflé glaze and band of incised foliate decoration, painted scissor mark, impressed 1912, 21 cm; above right: vase (shape 410) with mottled moss green soufflé glaze, dated 1914, 37 cm; below: three pieces featuring the mottled green-black soufflé glaze that remained in use until the 1920s, left to right, honey jar (shape 434) dated 1926, heavily potted vase, dated 1922, 28.5 cm, pot pourri in the form of a caddy (shape 362) with pierced rosettes, dated 1910, 21 cm.

These forms are hand-made on the potter's wheel under Mr. Taylor's supervision ; a specially prepared semi-vitreous clay of a light warm colour being used. They can be easily kept clean by dusting or washing, and the strong high lights and reflected lights of glazed earthenware so distracting in the early stages of form and light and shade teaching are avoided.

They are also specially adapted to the teaching of brush work and elementary design as applied to the enrichment of given forms, an important study in elementary and secondary schools and in the more advanced work of Schools of Art and Technical Schools. A skeleton decoration is painted on No. 17, as a suggestion. Corrections of pencil and water-colour designs can be made or the exercise removed by wetting so that the same shape may be used again and again, while approved designs can be rendered permanent by the use of wax, as in the encaustic painting of the Greeks.

A few smaller forms are shewn (A to G). These and a variety of other shapes (saucers, plates, and small vases) can be supplied with the vases at from 2d. to 6d. each, to be used as exercises in brush work for beginners.

The largest form is 10 inches in height.

Nos. 1, 3, 4, 5, 6, 8, 9, 11, 13, 14, 15, and 17   4/3 each nett.
Nos. 2, 10, 12, 16, 18, 19, 21, and 22   –   3/3   ,,
Nos. 7 and 20   -   -   -   -   -   2/3   ,,
The set of 22 vases   -   -   -   £3 12s. 6d. nett.

Packages and packing free on all orders of £2 and upwards.

Modelling clay 17/6 for 5 cwt. or 5/- per cwt. Packing extra.

Address :

W. HOWSON TAYLOR,
The Birmingham Tile and Pottery Works,
173, 174, Oldbury Road,
WEST SMETHWICK, BIRMINGHAM.

The above and also other forms glazed and enriched with colour and serving as examples for still life painting and as colour suggestion in design-ing can be obtained through the usual dealers. All glazes used contain no lead.

FORMS IN POTTERY

especially suited for teaching drawing and design, by

EDWARD R. TAYLOR,

Head-master of the Birmingham Municipal School of Art.

No. 2 as No. 3 but without handle. No. 4 as No. but 5 without handles. No. 8 as No. 9 but with two handles. No. 10 as No. 11 but with one handle. No. 16 as No. 17 but plain.

1 to 22 Registered.   All rights reserved.

'Forms in Pottery' leaflet, the pottery's first known catalogue, prepared by Edward Taylor and issued in about 1900.

simple four page folder printed in black that is headed *FORMS IN POTTERY, especially suited for teaching drawing and design, by EDWARD TAYLOR, Head-master of the Birmingham Municipal School of Art.* Dating probably from 1900 or 1901, this shows 22 vase and bowl shapes, with a selection of tableware, designed by Edward Taylor and made by W Howson Taylor, the Birmingham Tile and Pottery Works. The text on the leaflet makes it clear how these were designed to be used:

'These forms are hand-made on the potter's wheel under Mr Taylor's supervision; a specially prepared semi-vitreous clay of a light warm colour being used. They can be easily kept clean by dusting or washing, and the strong high lights and reflected lights of glazed earthenware so distracting in the early stages of form and light and shade teaching are avoided. They are also specially adapted to the teaching of brush work and elementary design as applied to the enrich-ment of given forms, an important study in elementary and secondary schools and in the more advanced work of Schools of Art and Technical Schools. A skeleton decora-tion is painted on No 17, as a suggestion. Corrections of pencil and watercolour designs can be made or the exercise removed by wetting so that the same shape may be used again and again, while approved designs can be rendered permanent by the use of wax, as in the encaustic painting of the Greeks. A few smaller forms are shewn (A to G). These and a variety of other shapes (saucers, plates, and small vases) can be supplied with the vases at from 2d to 6d each, to be used as exercises in brush work for beginners. The largest form is 10 inches in height.

Nos 1, 3, 4, 5, 6, 8, 9, 11, 13, 14, 15 and 17
    4/3 each nett
Nos 2, 10, 12, 16, 18, 19, 21, and 22
    3/3 "   "
Nos 7 and 20
    2/3 "   "
The set of 22 vases
    £3 12s 6d nett'

Equally important was a footnote stating that:

'The above and also other forms glazed and enriched with colour and serving as examples for still life painting and as colour suggestion in designing can be obtained through the usual dealers. All glazes used contain no lead.'

The idea of making ceramic forms specifically for use in the teaching of art students is naturally one that would have appealed to Edward Taylor and is something that would not, in any case, have been new to him, for a number of Victorian potters, for example, Minton, made similar wares. Included among the designs are shapes and styles of decoration previously included by Edward Taylor in his book *Elementary Art Teaching*. This is a vital document which not only reveals the philosophy behind the pottery during its early years, but also makes it clear that Edward Taylor was responsible for the design of shapes and decoration. As the author of the leaflet, he was also responsible for promotion and marketing, and it is in these areas that his contribution to the pottery's ultimate success was soon to become invaluable. Thanks to Edward's efforts, 1901 was to be a key year in the history of the pottery. The first exhibition of the products of the Birmingham Tile and Pottery Works was held at Smethwick Municipal School of Art during 1901, an event that must have been organised by Edward Taylor. Little is known about this exhibition, other than that the display included toilet sets, vases, tiles, jugs and small decorative pieces intended for mounting in silver. However, the exhibition may have inspired the pottery's first known press report, a long article published in *The Artist* in December 1901, under the heading 'Notes from Birmingham'. It is likely that Edward Taylor was, as ever, instrumental in the planning of this article as he would have been familiar with the magazine. Containing as it does so many clues about the pottery's early history, this article is worth quoting in full:

'*Notes from Birmingham*

Truly the crafts are making wonderful strides among us. We spoke last month of the artistic silver-ware which has so rapidly achieved widespread popularity and which has its source in Birmingham; now in addition to this a most interesting industry has sprung up and promises to flourish under the personal supervision of the headmaster of the Birmingham School of Art, Mr Edward R Taylor, and his son Mr Howson Taylor. The latter who is at any rate the nominal owner of the business, styles himself "a maker of decorated tiles, earthen-

ware and special ware for silversmiths," he might truthfully and justly add "also a designer of beautiful shapes, dainty patterns and charming colour schemes" and inasmuch as these effects are procured with leadless glaze and the workers are paid a day wage instead of by the piece, a humanitarian to boot.

It is however, purely with the artistic side that we propose to deal in this short note.

The factory in which all the work is done by hand, supplemented only by absolutely essential machinery and furnaces, is now in smooth working order. This is the outcome of almost herculean labour on the part of Mr Taylor, who during the last School of Art vacation assisted his son to watch the clay unceasingly and destroy hundreds of articles, which were not correctly patterned by the decorators, girls specially trained on the premises, or had accidentally lost their perfect form. The shape of the pottery is obtained indeed by the most minute attention and experiment; not made as in most works to a design previously set down on paper, nor in any way as a result of chance, but thrown off at the exact moment when the clay has assumed beautiful and useful proportions. A great advantage is thus gained over the ordinary producer to whom such a method of working would be a practical impossibility. The shapes, once originated, are of course repeated many times, "it is only the first step that costs."

This enterprise is on so important a scale that we are glad to see that the commercial side is by no means ignored: a show-room has been opened in the town and we were enabled to see there some very choice finished ware. There were, among other things, beautiful little scent bottles, well-shaped claret jugs and some salad-bowls conspicuous for their charming broken colour, all waiting to be mounted in silver or copper. This "broken colour" is a most interesting feature, it must not be confounded with the iridescent effects which William Morris so strongly condemned on the ground that they suggested decomposition. It is altogether more intentional and direct. It would perhaps be more right in many cases to speak of it as tone, a quality which is far too often entirely lacking, as a rule we see garish colour and no tone, here we have harmonious colour most expressively modulated. So varied and lovely is it that we find it difficult to credit the fact that owing to the leadless glaze and the consequent great heat required in firing, the makers are limited to three or four colours.

The hand-painted decoration is never heavy – generally some little floral motive is introduced – but it is always significant and it has this great advantage over much of the trade pottery, it is permanent and will last as long as the ware. It is incorporated with the glaze, instead of being put on in the customary way and fired at a lower heat with the customary or rather inevitable result that it wears off in time.

But the superiority of this hand-made work demonstrates itself in every direction; in handling the pottery we found that it was more delicately light than any china except the actually genuine egg-shell.

Many of the articles are of course complete without mounting of any sort, flower pots, tea sets, butter dishes, jugs, basins, bowls etc, etc, but it is in the goods prepared for silversmiths and in the ornamental tiles that there is perhaps the biggest future. Always on the alert, Messrs Haseler and Messrs Liberty have already secured many objects for mounting, as the possibilities revealed for table and other decoration in this combination of rarely beautiful colours and truly artistic mountings are practically limitless.

The tiles have much the quality of rich translucent enamel, some are merely displays of colour, without decoration of any kind, while others afford scope for really effective designs. A good opportunity manifests itself in this connection for the employment of students of the School of Art, where decorative leanings are always encouraged and fostered by the headmaster.

It is highly probable that some are already so employed, since no one is more anxious to promote the welfare of individual students than Mr Taylor. His indomitable energy on their behalf will be remembered gratefully by very many students in their after careers. We hope from time to time to see fresh designs in this beautiful pottery ware, which after much tentative and anxious work is now well advanced on its way to success.'

Particularly important in this article is the emphasis on the role of Edward Taylor, a point underlined in subsequent articles, along with details of production methods, the glazes used ('the makers are limited to three or four colours'), styles of decoration and the range of wares being made ('flower pots, tea sets, butter dishes, jugs, basins, bowls etc'). However, the most significant comments are those relating to wares for metal mounting and tiles:

> '...it is in the goods prepared for silversmiths and in the ornamental tiles that there is perhaps the biggest future.'

Clearly, the Taylors must have been producers of tiles and wares for metal mounting, following routes already known to be lucrative, and well trodden by other potters. William Moorcroft, for example, estimated in 1913 that one third of his annual turnover came from sales to electro-platers and jewellers. Yet, as ever in this early period the problem with the Taylors is that there are very few wares to support the documentary evidence. As stated earlier, tiles seem very rare, and only one metal mounted piece of this period, a silver mounted inkwell with a 1901 hallmark, has been recorded. From the evidence one has to assume that both tiles and metal mounted wares were made in quantity, but actual examples are rare today.

The Smethwick display was also important in establishing an exhibition policy, and from this date onwards the Taylors made a point of using exhibitions as a means of promoting their products. It is not known how many they attended before 1903, but there could have been several, often of a local nature. For example, there is a report, published in the January 1903 issue of the *Art Workers Quarterly*, of the 5th Exhibition of the Bristol and Clifton Arts and Crafts Society, held the previous October:

> 'In "Pottery", Messrs W & H Taylor of Birmingham carried off the first and second certificates with two fine examples of their "Ruskin" ware (metal cleverly used in conjunction) ...'

Apart from anything else, this report reveals that the Taylors had begun to use the Ruskin name by 1902. Exhibition successes may also have made clear to the Taylors the need for a permanent showroom apart from the pottery, and to this end suitable premises were found and equipped at 45 Newhall Street, Birmingham. The key exhibition of this period was, of course, that held in Paris in 1900, an international display that was to have a lasting influence on the decorative arts throughout the world. The Taylors did not show their wares, but they may have visited Paris, in which case there would have been ample opportunity for William Howson to study the fine displays of high temperature flambé wares by the French artist potters of the period, notably Dalpayrat.

Edward Taylor's other great achievement in 1901 was to persuade the Victoria & Albert Museum in London to buy some examples of Ruskin Pottery for their permanent collection. From the documents that survive it is apparent that it was Edward Taylor who made the approach. On 18th December 1901 he wrote to Mr Purdon Clark at the museum as follows:

'I have today sent some of our examples by passenger train & hope to have the pleasure of seeing you on Friday. With many thanks. Yours sincerely, Edward R Taylor'.

This letter was written from the Highfield Road address rather than the pottery, but all subsequent correspondence came from Oldbury Road. On the next day 'A collection of modern earthenware (47 pieces) also 12 tiles. On approval' was received at the museum and then delivered four days later to Bernard Rackham in the ceramics department. The same day a selection from the wares was made by Mr Crane, who chose the items he considered 'to be the most successful in form, colour and quality of glaze and pattern' and in due course the Museum purchased for £6.4s four vases, two bowls, a salad bowl, two cups and saucers, a bread and butter plate and an inkwell. The remaining wares were returned to the factory. Among those not selected were vases ranging in price from 4s to £1.5s, a covered marmalade at 8s, a tobacco jar at 10s, an olive dish at 5s, three jugs from 3s to 7s, a teapot at 12s, a large dish at £1 and a mustard pot at 4s, along with the 12 tiles.

Both the list of wares submitted on approval, and those purchased by the Museum, which are still in the collection today, provide vital clues to the production of the early years. Being fully priced, the list indicates not only the range of wares in production at the time, but also the pottery's cost structure. It is this document, and the price lists published in various exhibition catalogues over the next few years, that puts into doubt the whole financial structure of the pottery. With its small workforce, limited output and relatively low prices, the pottery could never have made the huge sums required either to repay Edward Taylor's initial investment or to maintain the Taylor family's standard of living over a long period. The Victoria & Albert Museum pots themselves are simple and unremarkable pieces, distinguished by their mottled blue, green and brown glazes, and sometimes revealing glaze and firing problems. Only the salad is unusual, with an orange glaze and a band of green foliate decoration round its shoulder. It would seem therefore that this small group of wares is entirely representative of the three or four glazes mentioned in the article in *The Artist*, and typical of the pottery's production at this period, with its dependence upon the blue/green chrome 11 glaze. The pieces are either unmarked, or carry the painted scissors or the impressed TAYLOR or WHT monogram marks. This documentary group of wares, all produced by 1901, offers a unique insight into the pottery's early years.

Little is known about the next year, 1902. Presumably the Taylors continued to expand their sales to retail outlets and to exhibit their wares at Arts and Crafts exhibitions around the country. The staff was not greatly increased, Florence Tilley's younger sister Beatrice having joined in 1901, at the age of 13, along with one or two other shadowy figures such as Percy Carol. William Howson was by now working on both the high temperature flambé and the lustre glazes but it is unlikely that either were in production. The local brown 'tocky' clay was given up, replaced by a porcelaineous stoneware specially made for the pottery by the Staffordshire suppliers, Wengers, and described as a mixture of ball clay, china clay, stone and calcined flint. Suitable for high temperature firing, this, introduced at least by late 1901, was to become the standard clay body at the factory for the rest of its life. It may also be that during this period the Taylors were deciding to concentrate on art pottery at the expense of tableware and tiles, even though both probably remained in production for some time to come.

Chapter V
1903-1908 – A PERIOD OF CONSOLIDATION

In January 1903, the *Pottery Gazette* published a long article about the Ruskin Pottery, describing the history of the business, its range of wares and the coloured glazes in use, and at the same time stressing the importance of Edward Taylor's role in the enterprise. Somewhat expanded and given a more localised context, this article was reprinted in the *Birmingham Daily Post* under the heading: A Birmingham Art Industry. The publication of this article may well have been inspired by Edward Taylor's forthcoming retirement from the Birmingham Municipal School of Art. Free now to devote his considerable energies to the pottery, his increased involvement can be measured by the much expanded programme of exhibitions, advertising and reviews from this period. The full text is as follows:

'The man who is successful in introducing a new industry to a great city should at least be placed on an equal footing, as a public benefactor, with the one who amid rural surroundings makes two blades of grass grow where one grew before. Hearty sympathy may therefore be accorded to Mr E. R. Taylor, the headmaster of the Municipal School of Art, in an enterprise in which he has been recently engaged, in association with his son, Mr Howson Taylor, for establishing here a manufacture of a new kind of artistic pottery. The circumstances which give rise to the development of a special industry in a particular locality are often peculiar. The presence of a number of small streams in the vicinity of Redditch, affording motive power in the days before the invention of the steam engine, led to the growth of that needle and fish-hook industry which is now of world-wide reputation; while the smiths who congregated in this free town in byegone days, aided by the iron and coal supply of "the Black Country", laid the foundation of the Birmingham hardware trades. The North Staffordshire Potteries seem to have developed in their particular neighbourhood, together with clay suitable for making the "saggars" in which earthenware and china are baked. The material of which plates and cups and vases are made is, for the most part, imported from other neighbourhoods, and with the increase of facilities for obtaining the materials for artistic pottery, there is no reason why an art pottery industry might not be established anywhere. Up to recently, however, we believe this kind of work has not come nearer to us than Stourbridge or Bilston.

It may not be generally known that Mr E. R. Taylor's father – the late Mr William Taylor, was an earthenware manufacturer at Hanley. Mr E. R. Taylor had, therefore, the opportunity for obtaining some knowledge of the processes of the craft before his love of drawing and painting led him into the ranks of Art teachers, in which he has achieved such conspicuous success. It was one of those natural reversions which doubtless turned his mind back to his father's pursuits. Upon the Continent, and particularly in France, there has been an immense amount of experiment in ceramics during the last few years and while it has led to some extravagances, it has also evolved some very beautiful productions. Mr Taylor's essays have had for their object the bringing out by handwork of the possibilities of the material manipulated, alike in form, and especially in colour. His first experiments, conducted at his house in Highfield Road, met with so much success that he was encouraged to set up a manufactory at West Smethwick; and a small show room at 45 Newhall Street, where the products of his wheel and furnace have been inspected by a large number of persons, and have received commendatory notice from several Art publications.

The "Ruskin Pottery" as the new ware has been christened, is shown in a great variety of forms, from tiles for fire-grate fittings to dainty little tea-cups, and scent bottles. Every article, from the largest to the smallest, is fashioned upon the potter's wheel and is free from any mechanical process, and from all imitation of what it is not. The decoration is under-glaze and takes the form either of free brush drawing in simple but graceful designs, or of a secret manipulation of the coloured glazes and of the firing, which results in some singularly beautiful mottled effects. Many of these resemble the markings of Mocha stones and Madrepores, but are not intentional efforts to mimic these. Deep blues and greens, and blueish grays appear to be Mr Taylor's favourite tints, and these seem specially suitable for grate tiles, for rose bowls and flower vases. The lustrous face of the tiles glows with ruddy reflection when there is a fire in the grate, but when there is no fire the green or blue face affords a cool decoration, while similar colours as applied to flower vases afford an effective background to the more vivid tints of the flowers themselves. Simple hues are employed for some very delicate tête-à-tête tea services. The articles in these instances are not only charmingly shaped, but are very thin, light, and smooth to the touch. Pale apple green and a sort of custard yellow tint are among those which are singularly refined, and with appropriate surroundings no less effective. Beauty of design, combined with beauty of colour, seems to be Mr Taylor's watchword. A new departure is the preparation of small round plaques – "roundels", varying from about three inches in diameter to the size of a small button. These are intended to be introduced as gems or points of colour in decorative woodwork and metal work. The glazes employed are all leadless, but require firing at a higher temperature than ordinary pottery. It is difficult to convey an adequate impression of the new ware in mere words. We have not, in this country, at any rate, seen anything better in the way of broken colour combined with a smooth surface, and a brilliancy approaching that of enamel. There is every reason to anticipate that the success already obtained may lead to further developments at the hands of Mr Taylor, or of other workers in the same department.'

This article gives an indication of changes taking place in the factory, namely the formal use of the Ruskin Pottery title, the expanding range of coloured glazes and a new departure, 'the preparation of small round plaques, "roundels" ... to be introduced as gems or points of colour in decorative woodwork and metal work'. While tiles and tablewares were still important, it was these roundels that were to become a major part of the pottery's output over the next few years, along with buttons. The inspiration for the article may have come from the Taylors' impressive display at the Arts and Crafts Exhibition Society's 7th Exhibition, held at the New Gallery in London in January 1903. The catalogue lists vases, bowls, tableware, jugs, a loving cup, a biscuit jar and tiles, exhibited by W Howson Taylor and executed by W Howson Taylor, William Forrester and Emily Boswell. Prices ranged from 2s 6d to £1.10s. The display was well received by the critics: 'In the pottery, Mr W Howson Taylor's work is conspicuous by its splendid colour' (*Art Workers Quarterly*). 'Mr Howson Taylor shows a few tiles and a quantity of pottery altogether admirable for the broken quality of its glaze' (The *Art Journal*). The *Pottery Gazette* continued to be enthusiastic, its reviewer giving a further description of the Taylor pieces in the April issue: '... the ornamentation of these pieces is characterised by great freedom, a quality that was not a feature of all the exhibits. We shall hope to see more of Mr H Taylor's work in the future.' The same issue of the *Pottery Gazette* contained the first known advertisement for the factory, a simple quarter page typographical display headed, 'The Ruskin Pottery and Tiles, made by W Howson Taylor and Edward R Taylor ARCA' and incorporating a quote from the London *Morning Post*: 'The Taylor colours are as pure and good as any that have been produced.'

Also well received was the display of wares at an arts and crafts exhibition held at Alexandra Palace in London in June the same year, but the comments made by the *Art Journal's* critic reveal that, with the increasing emphasis on colour and form, the Taylors were moving away from the more casual and 'artistic' approaches of some of their contemporaries:

'The pottery sent by Mr Taylor. of Birmingham may seem almost too truly turned and evenly glazed to the lover of art in clay, and what we are shown might easier be taken, at first sight, for china or stone ware; but where finish is much admired there will be high praise for this work. There is a rare blue on the best of it, and most of the shapes are good.'

Other displays included one at an arts and crafts exhibition in Leicester in August and September 1904 which inspired a review in *The Studio* accompanied, for the first time, by an illustration of three pots. The same year the Taylors also showed their wares at exhibitions in Leeds and Glasgow. The latter, an exhibition of British Pottery held at the People's Palace during the latter part of the year, included 'forty-nine specimens of Ruskin ware, made by Edward R Taylor and W Howson Taylor'. Four of these were subsequently bought by the Glasgow Museum and Art Gallery, including a dark red flambé

glazed bowl, probably the earliest documented piece of Ruskin flambé to enter a public collection. Others showing at the exhibition included Wedgwood, Sir Edmund Elton and the Della Robbia pottery. The same year the City Art Gallery, Manchester purchased their first piece, a 12-inch lily vase in mottled soufflé colours, followed in 1905 by four further examples, including three flambés. In fact, over the next few years a number of museums in Britain made significant Ruskin purchases, including Liverpool and Nottingham, the latter buying some lustres of 1906 and 1908.

By far the most important event of 1904 was the international exhibition held in St Louis in the United States to celebrate the centenary of the Louisiana Purchase. The decision by the Taylors to send their pottery to so prestigious an exhibition reflects not only a new confidence in the quality and consistency of their products, but also a determination to enter the international market place. The impetus for this change of direction probably came from Edward Taylor, who had both the necessary connections and the time to ensure that all the complicated arrangements involved in taking part in such a grand event were carried through smoothly. All the pieces to be included in the display would have been despatched at least by March of 1904, and so they must have represented an important early group. Unfortunately, no detailed list of the pieces

RUSKIN POTTERY

ENAMELS AND BUTTONS.

AWARDED THE

GRAND PRIZE

ST. LOUIS, 1904.

W. HOWSON TAYLOR.

Works and Showroom:

RUSKIN POTTERY, WEST SMETHWICK,

Near BIRMINGHAM.

STATION—SPON LANE (L. & N W.R.)

ILLUSTRATED COLOURED SHEET ON APPLICATION.

Above: Three Ruskin soufflé glazed vases, shown in the Leicester Arts and Crafts Exhibition, 1904, and illustrated in The Studio.
Below: Ruskin advertisement published in the Pottery Gazette in November 1905.

sent to America has survived, but there are plenty of clues in the contemporary reports of the exhibition. Revealing are the descriptive paragraphs contained in the official report of the British displays at St Louis, published by the Royal Commission in 1906. In the Ceramics section, paragraph 380 states:

> 'In the "Ruskin" Pottery Mr Howson Taylor aims at procuring elegance of form, refinement of colouring and purity of glaze. His exhibit included vases, butter and fruit dishes, flower bowls, cups and saucers, biscuit jars, candlesticks, claret jugs etc., all made on the potter's wheel. In the decoration, pattern is sometimes used but it is always kept subordinate, the chief aim being the artistic treatment of oxides etc, with leadless glazes. Combinations of blues, greens and purples predominate, but there are also examples of peach-blow, yellow, greys, light greens, oatmeal, turquoise and other colours. Dead glazes and new effects of transmutation glazes in addition to sang-de-boeuf, robin's egg blue resembling cloisonné enamels in pattern and colour. The articles vary in thickness, some being as light as egg-shell porcelain.'

A shorter paragraph, number 166, was also included under the heading 'Original Objects of Art Workmanship':

> 'The aims of "Ruskin Pottery" are good potting, beauty of form, and schemes of rich or tender colouring. The shapes are all made on the potter's wheel, and are such as grow out of the process under artistic guidance; the forms are not marred by added excrescences. The colourings range from slightly broken single colours, to combinations of colours; the textures and patternings aim at rivalling Eastern cloisonné enamels.'

In this case the wares were described as 'Executed by W Howson Taylor, W Forrester and E Boswell'. Both paragraphs were based closely on the introduction to the Taylors' 1905 catalogue, but still offer important clues to the nature of the St Louis display.

Also useful are some of the press comments. As late as February 1906 the *Pottery Gazette* was still carrying St Louis reports:

> 'Among the newer developments in British ceramics is the "Ruskin Pottery" by Mr Howson Taylor, who sent a number of vases, cups and saucers, candlesticks etc. showing diverse and lovely effects obtained by well-designed and subtle shapes, broken tints of colour and variety of surface and

lightness of body and a limpid leadless glaze of fine quality. The artistic merit of Ruskin Ware is mainly due to the influence of Mr Edward R. Taylor late headmaster of Birmingham School of Art.'

Edward Taylor's role was clearly an important one, and it is significant that it was to him that Gilbert Redgrave wrote on 24th October, 1904, to announce the award of a Grand Prix for the display of Ruskin pottery. Luckily, this letter still survives, addressed to Edward R Taylor Esq, Edgbaston, Birmingham:

> 'Dear Mr Taylor,
> You have been awarded the *Grand Prix*, which is the same as Sèvres and Mintons: the *highest award*. I must own that you obtain this great triumph mainly because of the great admiration expressed by the oriental experts, especially the Japanese, for your colours and glazes. I did not myself anticipate more than the gold medal, though, when it came to the voting, you were quite at the top ... your loan had a freshness and novelty which quite took the jurors by storm. Indeed, the great authority on porcelain who came over specially from Japan, where he is a leading manufacturer of Satsuma Ware, Mr Yabu, said you had successfully reproduced some of the best glazes of the "Ming" dynasty.
>
> Wishing you all success in your enterprise. Believe me, Yours Faithfully Gilbert R Redgrave.'

Orientalists apart, it should not be overlooked that the secretary to the judges at St Louis was the writer and potter Charles F Binns, who subsequently reviewed the Ruskin display in glowing terms in the *Transactions of the American Ceramic Society*. Even more important were articles about Ruskin in the *American Pottery Gazette*, first by John A Service, the magazine's English representative, and then another by an unnamed writer who quoted the following from Binns' 'Lessons from the St. Louis Exhibition':

> 'The Ruskin Pottery is an illustration of the possibilities which lie in the daily occupation of the potter. As a French chef can evolve new dishes and subtle flavours from the ordinary contents of the pantry, so the skilled and enthusiastic potter needs not the discovery of new materials and processes, but from the treasury of a resourceful mind can bring new things out of the old ... This is the lesson of St Louis. Our art is infinite. We have Clay, Glaze, Colour and Fire. With these the creative mind can express itself ...'

The writer then went on to list potters who had proved the great possibilities of pottery as art, with Ruskin, Rookwood and the French master Deck as his examples. In his article, John Service listed again the Ruskin colours, adding a 'brilliant sealing-wax red, dappled-sky gray' and a 'mottled rose-du-Barry' to those noted by other critics.

Charles Binns became a keen Ruskin supporter, and his influence could well have helped the pottery establish its place in the American market. However, there does not appear to have been any direct contact between the two until the latter part of 1905. In October Edward Taylor wrote to him, enclosing a copy of the colour plates in the 1905 catalogue, and on 22nd November Binns replied, writing on the stationery of The New York State School of Clay-Working & Ceramics at Alfred University, of which he was the director:

> 'My dear Mr Taylor, I have your kind letter of 30th. ult ... Your wares possess more of the ceramic spirit than I have ever seen in an English production of this class. They appeal to me very strongly as to one who is jealous of the dignity of pottery ...'

In fact, the Taylors had been in contact with various American collectors and enthusiasts at least since 1904. In December of that year Howson Taylor received a letter from the noted New York collector Dr Hochheimer concerning a request for an example of Ruskin ware.

> 'I know you will send something characteristic of your best work and worthy to be placed in my collection which embraces one specimen of every known factory at present existing which produces artistic pottery, the specimen being the finest which that factory is capable of turning out.'

Dr Hochheimer went on to recommend suitable New York retailers, including Tiffany, Gilman Collamore, Davis Collamore, Bedell and B Altman, and noting that the last named were already selling Doulton's rouge flambé.

For a small and relatively little known company employing at the most ten people (Percy Holland having joined in about 1903), the St Louis award was indeed a major triumph, and its impact was both immediate and considerable. The pottery's profile was increased by a regular series of advertisements in the *Pottery Gazette* from 1905, all including the phrase 'Highest Award Grand Prize St Louis 1904' and all listing the main areas of production as Ruskin Pottery, Enamels and Buttons. The enamels were the plaques designed for inserting into wood or mounting in metal, a mainstay of the factory at least since 1901,

but the emphasis on buttons is new, suggesting a development designed perhaps to replace the earlier dependence upon tiles while using the same machinery. From 1905 buttons figure prominently in advertisements and by 1909 these include the bold claim, 'Buttons for Dresses &c. are now in great demand.' Press reports of the same period underline this, with comments such as the following: 'Buttons for ladies' dresses, hat-pins, studs, cuff-links and scarf pins are among his (W Howson Taylor's) specialities.'

The button trade had long been established in Birmingham. 'Brummagem buttons' were famous in the early part of the 19th century, and increasing mechanisation ensured that Birmingham remained the major button production centre in Britain. Even in the early days production was said to average 600 million per year. Ceramic buttons had, of course, been made also over a long period. Richard Prosser's dust pressing patent of June 1840 covered the production of buttons and mosaic tesserae as well as tiles, and Minton were certainly not alone in being major producers of ceramic buttons by the Prosser process in the 1840s and 1850s. Button making remained a large, but relatively unregarded part of the ceramic industry through the 19th century, and then flourished in a more obvious manner from the 1870s with the fashion for more decorative buttons. The Ruskin Pottery was able to benefit directly from this fashion, thanks to their range of coloured glazes, but they were by no means alone. The tile maker, Minton, Hollins and Co., for example, exhibited in 1919 'an interesting line of pottery buttons' along with a series of medallions suitable for mounting as brooches, and Moorcroft also made decorative buttons during the 1920s. The strength of this market is underlined by the continued inclusion of buttons and enamels for insertion in jewellery, metalwork and furniture in the list of products in the Ruskin Pottery's 1924 brochure.

The lack of information about St Louis makes it impossible to establish with any certainty the precise nature of the Taylors' display. Reduction fired glazes and high temperature flambés were clearly included and were important in determining the award of the Grand Prix. However, what cannot be established is whether this was the first display of such wares, or whether they had been in production since the latter part of 1903. It is worth remembering that Royal Doulton used the St Louis exhibition as the launch vehicle for their range of flambé wares, developed for them by Bernard Moore, and so Howson Taylor may well have decided to mark the first appearance of his pottery on the international stage with a similar, but even more spectacular, gesture.

The next major Ruskin display was the arts and crafts exhibition at Leeds, mentioned earlier. The catalogue for this does survive, and includes a list of the wares shown, with their prices, but unfortunately there are no descriptions of shape, colour or glaze. On show were tiles, buttons, vases, bowls, cups and saucers, candlesticks, ink pots, egg cups with stand, jam pots, a jug, a pot pourri mounted in silver, a puff box mounted in silver, a tea bottle and an electric bell push. A bowl and a vase had wooden stands, perhaps the start of a touch of orientalism that was to become increasingly characteristic of the Ruskin Pottery. Prices for the vases ranged from 3s to 60s, but the majority of the wares were under 15s. Only seven bowls and vases out of 36 were priced at £1 or over, and so it seems fair to assume that these were either high temperature flambés or other rare glazes.

The Leeds exhibition attracted considerable attention and a range of revealing reviews. Notable was that published in *Arts and Crafts*:

> 'The exhibition now in progress at the Leeds City Art Gallery is replete with encouragement for those who take a hopeful view of our art industries ... The palm for the display of ceramic art, however, we have no hesitation in saying, must be awarded to Mr W Howson Taylor, whose case of "Ruskin Pottery" is simply a revelation to one unfamiliar with the products of the factory; it would win him distinction in any exhibition in any country. Nowhere, aside from the old products of China and Japan, is the exhibit to be surpassed for elegance of forms, refinement of colouring, or purity of glaze.'

The reviewer then goes on, interestingly, to compare the Ruskin versions of 'the wonderful old Chinese "flambé" and "soufflé" effects' with those made by Haviland of Limoges, making the point that while the Haviland examples were technically better, the Ruskin ones were much cheaper, and thus accessible to a far wider market. Also in the same exhibition was a case of Pilkington's Royal Lancastrian pottery, presumably wares with coloured glazed effects based on William Burton's researches, and these were priced from 21s to 105s, underlining once again the uncommercial nature of the Taylors' business at this time. Another exhibitor at Leeds was W C Gibson of Newcastle-upon-Tyne, who used the exhibition to launch their Adamesk ware which featured coloured leadless glazes derived from copper, cobalt, titanium and manganese, and fired in a muffle kiln at about 1200 degrees C. The greens, blues, yellows and bronzes of these wares must have been quite similar to the glaze effects achieved by the Taylors, and certainly shared the same basic technology. Also present were Royal Doulton and the Della Robbia Pottery.

The enthusiasm for glaze effects was widespread among British art potters at this time, inspired in part by the extensive technical literature then available. A key work was W J Furnival's *Researches on Leadless Glazes*, published in 1898, a book that may well have been in the Taylors' library, along with many detailed studies of oriental glazes by scholars such as Gulland. With this wealth of both stylistic and technical information readily available, it is surprising that Howson Taylor had apparently to devote so many years to experimentation. Some of his contemporaries, notably Bernard Moore and the Burtons, seem to have had much less trouble in achieving colourful glaze effects, but Taylor may well have been limited initially by the use of local 'tocky' clay. Certainly progress seems to have been much quicker once the factory had switched to the specially prepared stoneware body. There is, of course, a distinction to be drawn between the relatively low temperature majolica-type coloured glazes used by many potters at the end of the 19th century to achieve interesting effects, and the far more demanding high temperature soufflés of potters such as the Taylors and the Burtons, glazes based entirely upon the limited range of oxides capable of withstanding and reacting to a high temperature firing. These oxides produced colour effects that were either under the glaze or incorporated within it, a technology mastered long before by Chinese potters, notably during the Qing dynasty. Chinese monochromes therefore provided a well-established model, and the colours achieved by the Chinese seem to have set a standard that Howson Taylor attempted to match. Although extremely rare in some cases, there are Ruskin equivalents of the following Chinese glaze colours and effects: iron red, peach bloom, cobalt blue, powder blue, clair de lune, yellow, celadon, turquoise, mirror black, matt black, aubergine, pink, brown, tea dust and robin's egg. Some are known only through one example, while others seem to have been made on a regular basis. In addition, there were many Ruskin colours not based directly on Chinese models, usually mottled effects achieved by mixing glazes or by overlaying one glaze upon another. What is certain is that experimentation was a continuing process, with Howson Taylor creating a range of extraordinary, and sometimes unique, glaze effects during the early years of this century, alongside a group of more stable, and thus more readily repeatable soufflé colours, for example the standard blues, greens, yellows, pinks, purples and turquoises. The rare, and hard-to-achieve, effects were priced accordingly, a pattern that was maintained as the high temperature flambés gradually took over from the experimental soufflés. The term soufflé, derived from the French *bleu soufflé*, used to describe the technique of blowing cobalt blue in powder form onto the glaze that was widely practised by the Chinese in the 18th century, was also used by Howson Taylor to describe his own glazes, even though they were sprayed rather than blown. Taylor's source may have been Gulland, but in any case it is the term he continued to prefer to describe the wide range of coloured glaze effects he perfected and maintained in production until his interests switched to lustres, high temperature flambés and, ultimately, crystallines.

The greatest achievement of this period is undoubtedly the development of the high temperature flambé glazes. It is not possible to establish exactly when the first of these wares were produced, but they must have been the product of a long period of experimentation dating back at least to the early years of the century. James Ruston has reported that Howson Taylor used a small coal-fired kiln built specially in the factory yard for his experiments, but this could only fire one piece at a time. Later, a larger kiln was built, with two fire mouths and a capacity for up to a dozen pieces, and it was in this that most of the flambés must have been produced.

Known generally as the red kiln, this was surrounded by secrecy with no visitor ever being allowed near it. All the glazes were prepared by Howson Taylor himself and he also took charge of the long firing cycle which started at about 4am and then continued into the afternoon and evening. Clearly others must have been involved in the flambé firings, but it is hard to establish the exact roles of various members of staff. Apart from Edward Taylor, who obviously was in the know, the main helper seems to have been Ernest Porter, the placer and fireman, and thus the man employed to carry out exactly this kind of activity. Others who may have been associated with this work include Jack Cooksey, Florence Tilley and Howson Taylor's sister Nelly, although lack of technical knowledge might seem to make some of these rather unlikely candidates for so specialist a task.

With the lack of any detailed documentation, it has to be assumed that Howson Taylor used the oriental method of transmutation firing whereby copper-based oxides in suspension were applied to the biscuit wares, by painting or spraying, and then fired in an atmosphere in which the amount of oxygen was reduced in a controlled manner. The firing temperature was likely to have been between 1300 and 1600 degrees C. The startling effects of red, green, purple and yellow achieved by this process were highly varied and hard to predict, being dependent upon precise temperature control and the amount of smoke created during the reduction firing. Placing in the kiln was also very important. Inevitably, this complex technology produced unpredictable results and Howson Taylor, like all his contemporaries working in the same field, must have been faced with considerable wastage. Many high fired flambé wares exhibit clear signs of kiln damage such as cracking and surface flaws, and irregular bases caused by movement during firing. Glazes often flowed down to pool around the base, and grinding off the surplus was not unknown.

The first saleable flambés may have been produced in 1903, and certainly by March 1904 the process was sufficiently developed for examples to be sent to St Louis. From this date onwards flambés were included in all exhibitions, their presence clearly indicated by their high price structure. The first dated pieces known today carry the year mark for 1905, and it is apparent from these and from other evidence that flambé firing was by then fully under control. Flambé glazes were eventually applied to all manner of wares, from tiny miniatures to vases over two feet high, to tablewares, scent bottles, bowls, table lamps, jewellery enamels, plaques and buttons and even to patent inkwells. These early flambé pieces are marked by a richness of colour and a variety of technical control that puts them apart from those made later. Notable particularly is a range of wares marked with a distinctive snake-skin veining.

The Ruskin Pottery came of age between 1903 and 1908. Markets were expanding in response to exhibition successes and there is a definite aura of confidence. New staff were recruited, including Harry Hill, to help with clay preparation, and Andrew Forrester. The latter, William Forrester's nephew and a turner and modeller, came, like so many others, from Wedgwood. A new backstamp was introduced, the impressed oval containing the words Ruskin Pottery West Smethwick, and this was used with greater consistency even though the earlier marks, the WHT monogram and the painted scissors, did not entirely disappear. Impressed dating was used also from 1905. Inspired by the new Trade Marks Act, the Taylors also attempted to formalise the Ruskin name by writing to Mrs Joan Ruskin Severn to ask for permission to register it, but at this time the approach was not successful. However, Ruskin remained in use, replacing completely all earlier trading names. Much of this must have been due to the organisational abilities of Edward Taylor, able now to devote all his

ILLUSTRATED CATALOGUE

OF

RUSKIN POTTERY

MADE BY

W. HOWSON TAYLOR

(Member of the London Arts and Crafts Exhibition Society),

AND

EDWARD R. TAYLOR, A.R.C.A., London

(Late Head Master of the Birmingham Municipal School of Art).

Works and Showrooms:

RUSKIN POTTERY,

WEST SMETHWICK,

near BIRMINGHAM,

ENGLAND.

(STATION: Spon Lane, L. & N.W.R.)

(Electric Trams from near Birmingham Town Hall pass the works.)

AWARDED A

GRAND PRIZE

(Highest Award)

AT THE

St. Louis International Exhibition,
1904.

Exhibited at the principal Art Galleries and Arts and Crafts Exhibitions.
Agents in London, the provinces and abroad.

(Price One Shilling, returned on orders of £1 and upwards.

Title page of the Ruskin 1905 catalogue.

time to the running of the factory and the promotion of its products.

There can be no doubt that the hand of Edward Taylor can also be seen very clearly in the pottery's first proper catalogue, issued during the summer of 1905. This is an impressive document, with a stiff cover, two colour plates of groups of ware and an illustration of each of the 255 shapes then in production, along with size and price codes, and details of the three marks then in use. Included are long extracts from recent press notices of exhibition displays but most important of all is the introduction, a clear and concise statement of intent by the Taylors. This is vital in establishing the philosophy, design principles and aims of the Ruskin Pottery, and so is printed below in full.

'The aims of Ruskin Pottery are good potting, beauty of form and rich or tender colourations.

Good potting means a sound body and delicate workmanship, and such a coating of glaze as makes the ware as delightful to handle as to look at. Some bowls are as light in weight as old egg shell porcelain.

The shapes are all made on the potter's wheel, and are such as grow out of the process under artistic guidance, and the forms are not marred by added excrescences.

The colourings range from slightly broken single colours, to combinations of colours; textures and patternings rivalling eastern cloisonné enamels, and suggestive of rich hues seen in rock pools by the sea.

No moulding, casting or machine processes are employed in the making, nor printing, lithographing or gilding in the decoration. When pattern is used, it is hand painted and kept subordinate, no attempt being made to paint realistically, flowers, landscapes or figures, nor to imitate old porcelain or pottery. The colours used are incorporated with the glaze and are therefore limited to the few oxides, &c., which will resist the great heat of the potter's oven, but the colour effects are almost unlimited, an expert stating that they are equal to those of the best period of the Chinese Myng Dynasty. These include our well-known blues, greens, purples, clair-de-lune, pink, crushed strawberry, yellow, turquoise, and combinations of these colours, also others which are more difficult to reproduce, as a special blue, robin's egg blue, sang-de-boeuf, peach bloom, lustres, crystallines, shagreen, bowls of egg-shell thinness, &c.; many being unique specimens.

The colourings harmonize with each other, and with flowers, fruit, silver and artistic furnishings.

Many letters of congratulations and praise have been received from artists and collectors, and purchases of the pottery have been made for Art Galleries and Museums.'

Entitled *Illustrated Catalogue of Ruskin Pottery Made by W Howson Taylor and Edward R Taylor ARCA London*, this document offers plenty of evidence to support the view that the business was at this time a partnership between father and son. With his proven design, publishing and administrative experience, Edward Taylor was ideally placed to plan and supervise the production of such a document. He may well have designed many of the shapes, building upon the foundation he laid down in the earlier *Forms in Pottery* folder, and the presentation of the material, the shape photographs, the numbering

W. HOWSON TAYLOR, Sole Maker of Ruskin Pottery, Enamels, and Buttons.

West Smethwick, BIRMINGHAM. Catalogue of the Pottery and Samples of Enamels for Insertion in Metals, Woods, &c., sent on Application.

(Station: SPON LANE (L.N.W.R., or Dudley trams to Spon Lane.)

Highest Award. Grand Prize, St. Louis, 1904.

Ruskin advertisement published in the Pottery Gazette, May 1906, from a series featuring illustrations from the 1905 catalogue.

system and the production control all reflect his orderly mind. Other clear indications of Edward Taylor's important role can be seen in one of the reviews printed in the new catalogue. Under the heading 'Two New Potters', the critic of the *Morning Post*, discussing, presumably, the London Arts and Crafts exhibition of 1903, wrote:

'... Anyone can make new pottery: a new potter is a thing to be thankful for. And it appeared that two, working in close and inseparable collaboration, were to be dealt with, whose productions possessed not only mere excellence of make, but a strong savour of individuality. Mr Edward R Taylor, the well known Principal of the Birmingham School of Art, has been able actually to attempt the realisation of one of the great desires of his life, the making of good pottery, in co-operation with his son, Mr W Howson Taylor.'

This review then described the quality and lightness of the potting, and the purity of the colours, mentioning 'a fine blue of quite uncommon quality ... a light peacock green; a peculiarly rich brown which combines finely with the darker blue; a canary yellow, used effectively with apple green and a soft Indian red ...' It is possible also to detect the presence of Edward Taylor in the rather emotive phrases used to describe the colours in the catalogue's introduction: 'textures and patternings rivalling eastern cloisonné enamels, and suggestive of rich hues seen in rock pools by the sea.' It is not just that Taylor obviously wrote these words; more important is the way they capture the spirit of the age and underline the links between Birmingham School of Art and the Newlyn School painters, many of whom had been Taylor's pupils. The impact of the seaside, and the effects of light and colour were primary interests among late Victorian artists, and so the link between these contemporary ideas and the abstract, broken colours and reflective

surfaces of the Ruskin pots has to be Edward Taylor, even if it was his son who actually created the glazes.

The 1905 catalogue is very revealing about Ruskin production of this period, including as it does photographs of a wide range of wares. Vases, covered vases, bowls and covered jars predominate, but also shown are cheese and cake stands, tea caddies, jugs, candlesticks, a porringer and a loving cup, pot pourris, ink pots, a trinket set, an egg stand, a covered muffin, sweet dishes, miniatures, a cress bowl and stand, stands for oil lamps, and even an electric bell push and some door knobs, along with pieces made for metal mounting. Not shown but mentioned are tablewares, altar vases, enamel plaques and buttons, all known to have been in production at this time. Shapes are numbered in sequence, but the shapes are not necessarily related to each other even though some grouping does occur. The catalogue clearly does not show all the shapes, for a number of pieces are known from this period with shape numbers in the 400s. Presumably these are legacies from some earlier system of shape numbering. In principle, as the numbers from 1905 are sequential, they can provide a rough indication of the date of introduction, at least until 1912. Shapes appear to have been introduced in batches over this period, and those which were successful in commercial terms, became part of the standard range while those which failed simply were not repeated. Equally, shapes which had initially had a short life could at a later date be resurrected, perhaps in another size or with a different glaze finish. Inevitably, there were many more shapes associated with the factory than were ever in production at any one time, and so it is not surprising to find that many of the shapes illustrated in the 1905 catalogue have never been seen by collectors today.

The catalogue specifically mentions lustres among the list of glazes in the introduction, and the colour plates certainly include lustred pieces, notably the soft yellow and orange type which is rather impermanent, the dark kingfisher blue and the standard soufflé colours with an additional lustre finish. The inspiration for lustre production came initially from the work of 19th-century pioneers such as William De Morgan, Cantagalli, Carocci (at Gubbio), Ginori and Clement Massier. Also important were the lustres produced by Maws and Craven Dunnill, Shropshire companies not far from Smethwick. Both Walter Crane and Lewis F Day designed lustre wares for Maws, and their products were well known from both exhibitions and contemporary publications. While most of the 19th-century makers produced reduction fired ruby lustres in maiolica or Hispano-Moresque styles, there was some production of single colour work, notably some monochrome vases made at Craven Dunnill between 1880 and 1900 with lustre finishes in blues, greens and violets. These pieces are quite close to what the Taylors were making 20 years later. Also important was William Burton, who started glaze trials for lustres at Pilkington in January 1903. Pilkingtons first showed their lustres in London in January 1906, and by this time lustres were also in production at Poole. Readily available was a wealth of technical information. In November 1899 *The Artist* had published detailed directions for the preparation of ceramic lustres, but these were based largely on lead. More relevant perhaps was the section on On-Glaze Decorative lustres included by W J Furnival in his *Leadless Decorative Tiles, Faience and Mosaic*, published in 1904. By this time, ready-made lustre glazes were obtainable, many coming from French and German suppliers, and a number of British potters were experimenting in this field. Further information was available in a number of technical manuals, for example Rudolph Hainbach's *Pottery Decorating*, published in London in 1907, which included an extensive chapter on contemporary lustres, complete with recipes. With this background, it is not surprising that the Taylors chose to add lustres to their range of coloured glazes in 1905. As so often with Ruskin, the actual pieces no longer seem to exist, with very few lustres known today that predate 1908. A notable exception is a yellow lustre vase dated 1906, in the collection of Glasgow Museum and Art Gallery. However, this early and perhaps experimental work established a pattern of lustre production that was to be greatly expanded from about 1908.

Another important development of the 1904 to 1906 period was the growth of the Taylors' export business. There are various references that suggest the increasing significance of the United States market, but actual evidence is hard to come by. In December 1905 Howson Taylor was elected a member of the Arts and Crafts Society of Boston, Massachusetts, but it is not known whether he exhibited regularly at shows organised by this and other North American societies. Certainly high temperature Ruskin flambés were on display in Tiffany's in New York in October 1907, reflecting a pattern of selling through major North American retail outlets. It is tempting to speculate that the relative shortage today of Ruskin pottery of this period in Britain is because so much was sent overseas. Certainly the export business during this early period became the foundation upon which the pottery's stability was to rest in later years. It may also be significant that Florence Tilley, the factory's first employee, left in 1905 or 1906 and went to live in America. Her reasons may well have been personal, because of the difficulties that had arisen from her friendship with Howson Taylor, but she could also have worked in some representational or promotional capacity.

The need to look beyond the shores of Great Britain was also underlined by an expanded programme of exhibition displays. At the International exhibition in Milan in 1906, the Ruskin Pottery, one of the few British companies taking part, gained a second Grand Prix and the accolade of *The Studio* which reported 'a remarkable case of Ruskin Pottery'. At Christchurch in New Zealand the following year the award was a Grand Prix Hors Concours, suggesting perhaps that one of the Taylors may have been a member of the organising committees or the jury. As with St Louis, the awards at Milan and Christchurch were featured on advertisements, promotional literature, and the labels attached to the bases of the pots. In Britain, another new venue was the annual exhibition of the Home Arts and Industries Association. The Taylors first exhibited in May 1905 at London's Albert Hall, and their wares prompted this response from the critic of the *Art Workers Quarterly*:

> 'Mr Taylor does not attempt pattern in any form, but relies for effect on broken colour harmonies, and in this direction it would be difficult to conceive anything more beautiful than the examples he showed.'

The review then went on to comment unfavourably on the shapes, the writer clearly preferring 'Old Greek and Etruscan vase forms'! Ruskin pottery continued to be shown at this event for some years.

However, in Britain the main event of this period was probably the Arts and Crafts Exhibition Society's 8th show, held in London in January 1906. The Ruskin display included a range of vases and bowls, 'by W Howson Taylor, E R Taylor and assistants,' and, judging by the prices which ranged from 8s 6d to £15, the emphasis was now on high temperature flambés and rare glaze effects. It was from this exhibition that the Victoria and Albert Museum made its next major Ruskin purchase, buying two shape 96 bowls and a shape 354 vase for a total of £16 10s. All are high fired flambés, and together they reveal the enormous improvement in quality and finish that had been achieved by the Taylors since the museum's first purchase in December 1901. The vase bears a 1905 date, but the bowls are undated. All three came with hardwood stands. At the same exhibition, the Museum also purchased four monochrome glazed bowls and vases from the Pilkington display, wares now noticeably cheaper than the Ruskin pieces. *The Studio*, reviewing the exhibition, commented:

> 'Pottery has never been so well represented ... and it is respectively to Mr Howson Taylor and the Pilkington Tile Company that the credit is chiefly due.'

The reviewer also commented on the scattered Ruskin display, with pieces in different rooms shown

Group of high-fired and lustre wares illustrated in The Studio Yearbook, 1908.

The Ruskin stand at the Ideal Home Exhibition, 1908, illustrated in the Pottery Gazette, December 1908.

along with work by artists so diverse as Ernest Gimson and W A S Benson. This appears to have been a characteristic of the Arts and Crafts Society's exhibitions.

In 1907 the *Art Journal* noted:

> 'an exhibition of china and earthenware finished with leadless glazes, held at the Church House, Westminster, should forward the movement against the employment in potteries of a material dangerous to life ... to buy and use ware which is produced safely is no longer a moral act implying aesthetic renunciation.'

The Taylors took part, along with Pilkington and Royal Doulton.

The next important event was the Franco-British Exhibition, opened by the Prince and Princess of Wales in pouring rain on 14th May 1908. It was held in west London and arranged in a series of dazzling white pavilions that gave the area its new name, White City. Ruskin wares were displayed at this exhibition, the *Pottery Gazette* finding it curious that they were on show, not as might be expected in the Palace of Decorative Art, but in the Palace of Women's Work:

> '... He (Howson Taylor) also exhibits a collection of his very pretty "Ruskin" buttons for ladies' dresses – perhaps these account for his artistic pottery being found among the flounces and furbelows. Still, wherever it may be shown, "Ruskin Pottery" will command appreciation for its genuine artistic excellencies.'

The *Gazette* was clearly not alone in this view, for Howson Taylor gained his third Grand Prix at this event. The same year Ruskin Pottery was on show at the *Daily Mail's* Ideal Home Exhibition, again somewhat unexpectedly displayed among the textiles. The *Pottery Gazette's* review, published in December 1908, confirms the new emphasis on lustre:

> 'He has been for some time experimenting with special metallic colours fired at high temperatures, and, like other chemist-potters, he has produced some beautiful effects.'

The photograph accompanying the review shows the increased emphasis on both lustres and high fired flambés at the expense of the standard soufflés. Tantalisingly, this review also mentions crystalline effects, meaning perhaps the brown aventurine glaze then in use.

The increasing emphasis on the high fired production was also underlined by the wares illustrated in magazines. Groups of Ruskin flambé pieces appeared in the *Studio Yearbook of Decorative Art* every year from 1906 to 1908, while the *Art Journal's* three-part series on British pottery by John A Service, published in 1908, included photographs of 11 Ruskin high temperature wares, and one large lustre bowl, along with examples by contemporaries such as Moorcroft, Pilkington, Bernard Moore and Royal Doulton.

In 1906, or thereabouts, the 1905 catalogue was revised and extended, to shape 326. Obviously by this time the shapes that did not sell were being abandoned, to be replaced by new ones that reflected more accurately the current enthusiasm for Chinese forms. This catalogue included a further 50 vases and bowls of general Chinese inspiration. Although the format of the catalogue remained the same, with pots photographed in rows, this new edition included also some that were patently drawings of the proposed shape stuck onto a backing sheet. This cheaper way of testing market response was far more noticeable in the next catalogue, a simple eight-page folder issued in about 1909. This includes more Chinese-style forms and takes the shape numbers to 353. However, by this time many of the earlier, less successful shapes were actually not in production. Gone, for example, are most of the bowls, the jugs, the tablewares and the covered jars, along with most of the small pieces which were clearly proving to be too uneconomical. This inevitable process of rationalisation reflects the more commercial and practical approach to pottery-making now dominant at Oldbury Road.

ENAMEL PLAQUES AND METAL MOUNTING

The use of semi-precious gemstones in secular and domestic metalwork is particularly associated with three designers, Charles Rennie Mackintosh, Charles Robert Ashbee and Archibald Knox. Generally, however, it is the work of Ashbee for his Guild of Handicraft and Knox for Liberty which set the fashion, and pieces of silverware dating from about 1900 establish the style. The preferred stones were turquoise, green chrysoprase, chalcedony and sometimes garnet, often combined with mother-of-pearl and enamels. The enamels featured complementary colours of green and red, or turquoise and orange. Inevitably, once the work of these designers was recognised, especially Liberty's widely publicised Cymric silver range, others followed, and similar designs are known from, among others, Arthur Gaskin, Bernard Cuzner and William Snelling Hadaway in the period 1902-05. In any case, publication in magazines such as *The Studio* ensured that the length of the time between innovation and copying was short.

FLAMBÉ WARES c1903-1914

Three sang de boeuf vases spanning the lifetime of flambé production. Left, vase (shape 390) with red clouding on a pebbled grey ground, illustrated in colour in the 1924 promotional brochure, 24 cm, dated 1924; centre, bottle vase (shape 219) with a sealing-wax red glaze, illustrated in colour in the 1905 catalogue, 17.5 cm, dated 1905; right, heavily potted vase 27.3 cm, dated 1933.

Above: a group of wares with a speckled green flambé glaze; left, caddy (shape 362 with additional knop on lid) with rare glaze known only on this example, 22 cm, dated 1926 and painted E141 (experimental glaze number); centre, vase (shape 271), 19 cm, dated 1906; right, vase (shape 318), 26 cm, illustrated in The Studio Yearbook in 1908.
Below: a group of wares with green and purple-mauve flambé glazes. Left, vase (shape 20), 21 cm, dated 1933; centre, vase (shape 328), 29 cm, dated 1909; right, caddy (shape 426), 11.5 cm, dated 1912.

Above: three flambé vases (shape 263 – originally shape 89), left, with fissured glaze, illustrated in the colour plates in the 1913 catalogue and the 1924 promotional brochure, 25 cm, dated 1910; centre, with red fissured glaze, 20.2 cm, dated 1911; right, with purple red streaked glaze, 20.2 cm, dated 1905. Below: vase (shape 215) with petal-effect glaze, 19.5 cm, dated 1905.

Above left: vase (shape 193) with reticulated green glaze on a purple and ivory ground, purchased by the Victoria & Albert Museum from the London Arts and Crafts Exhibition Society in January 1906, 16.5 cm, dated 1905 (Trustees of the Victoria & Albert Museum); above right: vase with banded red-green glaze, 16.6 cm, dated 1906; below: three wares with green flambé glazes, left, covered vase (shape 136), 18.5 cm, WHT monogram impressed, centre, vase (shape 100), 10.5 cm, WHT monogram impressed and dated 1905, right, vase (shape 67 or 77), 16 cm, painted scissors mark, dated 1905.

Above left: two frequently found early shapes, left, covered vase (shape 119), 27 cm, WHT monogram impressed, right, vase (shape 244), 22 cm, dated 1910; above right: vase (shape 27) 26.7 cm, impressed marks; centre left: vase with snake green flambé with diaperings, 38 cm, dated 1909, vase (shape 306) with blue-green diaperings, 22.5 cm, dated 1906, vase (shape 63) with purple-red diaperings, 25 cm, dated 1906; centre right: wares with black cherry flambé glazes, vase (shape 27), 26.5 cm, painted scissor mark, dated 1905, vase (shape 334), 22.5 cm, impressed marks; right: vase (shape 332), formerly owned by Howson Taylor's brother, pewter rim, 29 cm, dated 1907.

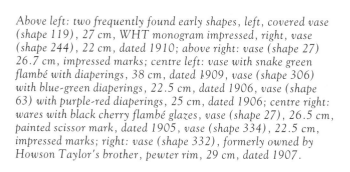

Covered vase (shape 119) with fissured blue-green glaze, 26.5 cm, impressed marks. This, one of the most famous of all Ruskin flambé glazed vases, was illustrated in The Studio Yearbook for 1907 and in the 1913 catalogue. One of only two examples with this glaze, it was displayed in a cabinet in Howson Taylor's sitting room until 1935. The second was bought by Count Kessler of Weimar.

Above: colour plates of flambé glazed wares from the 1913 catalogue and the 1924 promotional brochure.
Below left: vase (shape 20) with mottled red-purple snakeskin flambé glaze, 26 cm, dated 1913; below right: vase (shape 353) with banded red-purple flambé glaze, 29 cm, dated 1910.

Above left: vase (shape 55) with red-green fissured flambé glaze, illustrated in the 1913 catalogue, 19 cm; above right: two vases (shape 261) with rich red-blue flambé glazes, 21 cm, dated 1912 and 1909; below: wares with mottled red-green flambé glazes on ivory grounds, left, vase, formerly owned by Howson Taylor's brother, 21 cm, dated 1915, centre, vase (shape 292), 19.3 cm, dated 1909, right, vase (shape 341), 19.8 cm, dated 1908.

The stones used were not expensive, and most pieces produced in this style were in silver. Liberty used the services of a number of silversmiths to execute the designs and from 1901 established a manufacturing connection with W H Haseler of Birmingham. Liberty pioneered the use of pewter in their cheaper Tudric range introduced in about November 1901, which retained the style and designs of the Cymric range with great effect, the coloured stones and bright enamels blending particularly well with the soft sheen of the pewter surfaces.

The article on Ruskin published in *The Artist* of December 1901 included the sentence:

> 'Always on the alert, Messrs Haseler and Messrs Liberty have already secured many objects (of Taylor pottery) for mounting, as the possibilities revealed for table and other decoration in this combination of rarely beautiful colours and truly artistic mounting are practically limitless.'

These pieces would have been the wares designed for metal mounts, for it was not until 1903 that it was reported that 'a new departure (for Ruskin) is the preparation of small round plaques to be used as gems (for mounting in caskets etc).'

The predominant Ruskin Pottery soufflé colours of the period, green, blue, turquoise and purple, often intermingled to look even more like gem stones, would have encouraged their use. In addition, they had a great price advantage even over the 'cheap' semi-precious gemstones. However, it is relatively rare to find Ruskin Pottery gems used on silver, but their use with pewter and copper was widespread, not only on tablewares, caskets, mirrors, vases and so on, but also in jewellery.

Ruskin pottery plaques were made in a variety of shapes, including roundels of various sizes up to about three inches, hearts, squares, rectangles, diamonds and more complex quatrefoil and half moon shapes. Usually they are of fairly flat cross section but some cabochon examples are known.

Although Haselers were mentioned, no Ruskin plaques have been discovered in the Cymric and Tudric ranges. However, other Liberty makers may have employed them.

James Dixon of Sheffield used Ruskin Pottery plaques in their pewter range, as did another Sheffield maker, William Hutton, in silverware. However, the Birmingham firm most closely associated with the use of Ruskin pottery plaques was that of A Edward Jones who was associated with Jesson, Birkett and Company Ltd. Jones is thought to have mounted an inkwell in silver as early as 1901 when he was associated with the Birmingham Guild of Handicraft. Jesson, Birkett

Above: Jug with metal mounts, similar to one illustrated in the 1905 catalogue.
Below: Bowl with metal mounts in Art Nouveau style, additionally decorated with applied enamels, about 1905.

were formed in 1904 and registered their mark at Birmingham Assay Office on 17th February 1904. The *Art Journal* of 1905, states:

> 'In a measure of collaboration, as well as by the fact that they are fellow craftsmen of

Birmingham, Messrs Jesson, Birkett & Co. are connected with Howson Taylor, and in some of their metal caskets, on dials of clocks whose metal cases are the work of the firm, and employed in various forms of light and heat fittings of every kind, the potter's craft is well joined to the art of the metalworker.'

Jesson, Birkett also acted as London wholesale agents for the Ruskin Pottery at least from 1909, when their name appears on a Ruskin advertisement printed in the *Pottery Gazette*. Jesson, Birkett finished production when they went into liquidation in 1910. A Edward Jones, however, continued to the 1980s. Known pieces by Jones using Ruskin pottery include a silver teaset of 1908/09 which has a Ruskin Pottery stud for the finial of the teapot lid, and a range of wares with silver mounts of the period 1906 to 1910, featuring a variety of glazes, including flambé, a bowl of mottled blue and buff glazes with elaborate strapwork mounts of 1933, and similarly mounted bowls from 1935 which appear to have had a Celtic inspiration, with foot and collar engraved with decorative ropework bands linked by vertical hinged strapwork or interlaced wirework. Examples with three and five straps are known, not all by Jones, for Hicklenton & Phillips produced a similar design, also in 1935. Such pieces either represent stock held by the mounters for some time, or items bought in 1933/4 at the end of production.

Although there were about 20 shapes designed for metal mounting from the earliest period of the factory, very few examples with metal mounts are known. It is probably significant both from the point of view of Ruskin sales of such items and from the state of the metalworking trades as a whole that all such shapes were deleted from the Ruskin catalogue issued in about 1909. The last pieces with metal mounts, except for the bowls of the 1930s, seem to have been dated 1909 to 1910. Not all mounting of Ruskin Pottery, especially the plaques, is of this quality and the style could be copied by the Home Arts and Industries elements of the Arts and Crafts movement. Such pieces include boxes set with a roundel, with sheet pewter covering the wooden carcass, or simple pewter jewellery with Ruskin plaques.

The finest boxes with Ruskin Pottery gems were those produced by Jesson, Birkett & Co and A Edward Jones to designs by Annie G Stubbs (who had been a pupil at the Birmingham School of Art and who was married to Thomas Birkett), Florence Camm and Bert Harvey. These used the process of colouring copper developed by R Llewellyn B Rathbone, a relation of the metalworker W A S Benson. Rathbone's trademark of St Dunstan and the copper colouring process were acquired by the Faulkner Bronze Company, and by the time Faulkner retired the company had been reconstituted as Jesson, Birkett. At a later date, about 1905/06, A Edward Jones bought the rights to, or acquired an interest in, the St Dunstan trademarks, the colouring process and the Faulkner Bronze/Jesson, Birkett pattern book. The boxes were characterised by sheet copper bodies riveted with metal straps at every edge, and strapwork sometimes containing a Ruskin Pottery roundel, or roundels, often in blue and green colours. The hinged lids often extend beyond the sides of the box and the surfaces have the typical hand-hammered quality of this type of factory-made but hand-finished Arts and Crafts metalwork. The colours of the gems stand out particularly well against the tones, often bronze, though the process also gave brown, black, yellow, green, or blue, on the metal surface.

There appears to have been some kind of crisis in the Arts and Crafts metalworking firms from about 1908. Lack of orders for the metalworking shop was one of the chief reasons for the losses which closed Ashbee's Guild of Handicraft in 1908. Jesson, Birkett went into liquidation in 1910, while Liberty sold off their designs to other firms for cheaper production in 1909/10. Ashbee blamed Liberty, but the real reason was probably the horde of lady amateurs whose home-made handcraft swamped and undercut the professional manufacturers. Despite this, Ruskin continued to make gems and plaques at least until 1924, long after the fashion for such things had passed, and so it is not surprising that boxes of roundels, plaques and gems have survived, often in the families of former employees.

Chapter VI
THE PRE-WAR YEARS

In 1909 there were two international exhibitions at which Ruskin Pottery was on display. The Imperial International was held at the White City, London in July, but more important for the Taylors was the International Exhibition of the Fine Arts in Venice. In June 1909 the *Pottery Gazette* was able to report:

'... the Italian government have purchased several specimens of his Ruskin pottery ... These are acquired for the Museum of Industrial Art at Rome. We congratulate Mr Taylor upon this deserved recognition of his beautiful Art ware.'

The importance of such museum purchases was paramount, not just for the status they granted to the pottery, but also as a means of building up the crucial export business upon which the factory increasingly depended. North America was a major market, and it is possible that William Howson Taylor may have visited the United States before 1910. Promotion and sales apart, he had the additional attraction of Florence Tilley, by then resident there with her son.

Another exhibition in which the Taylors showed their wares was Modern English Pottery, held at the Queen's Park branch of Manchester City Art Gallery from September 1909. The introduction to the catalogue makes clear the aims of the exhibition, while emphasising the links between oriental inspiration and modern technology.

'The object of the present exhibition is to illustrate the ideals and aspirations that are guiding the production of the best decorative pottery in England today. We seem to be returning to the truer standpoint well known to the artists of byegone centuries, that every material should be used in such a way as best to display its special qualities. These are: 1. That the material from which it is fashioned is plastic, and is capable of receiving simple and elegant form under the hand of the workman; 2. That the glaze and colour are in themselves sufficiently beautiful, when rightly used, to make even simple pieces of pottery entirely beautiful ... Nothing is more striking in the present exhibition that the fact that the English potters ... have instinctively based the form of their vases, dishes, &c., on those of the Persian and Chinese potters of the Middle Ages ... Alongside the influence of this ancient Oriental Art there is also to be seen the influence of modern science applied to pottery glazes, and, whilst many of the examples shown recall the past, the greater number speak even more of the present when scientific knowledge has been called in to supplement, or extend, the work of the pottery decorator. The variety of glazes and of colours is astonishing in its range, and in these respects the present collection of modern English pottery is probably more representative than any which has been gathered together before.'

Besides the Ruskin Pottery, Pilkington, James Macintyre (showing pottery by William Moorcroft), Bernard Moore and Ashworth Brothers of Hanley, who used the exhibition to promote their new Estrella and Lustrosa ranges of lustre glazed wares, took part. Lustre was very much the style of the moment, and Howson Taylor was only one of a number of potters making the most of this particular bandwagon. Pilkington and Moorcroft had also introduced decorative lustres, and by July 1909 the Ruskin Pottery's advertisements were specifically mentioning 'coloured glazes and lustres'. The first Ruskin lustre colours were yellow, orange, grey and green.

In 1910 Manchester City Art Gallery bought five Ruskin pieces from the exhibition for their collection, including a ten-inch high fired flambé vase with a silver footrim dating from 1906/07. This shape, 272, was priced at £2. Others in this group include another flambé vase, shape 63, priced at £1.10s, a shape 40 yellow lustre bowl at 8s 6d, and two soufflé pieces, a vase and a bowl, at 7s 6d each. No less than 57 of the 68 items shown by Ruskin at Manchester were priced between 6d and 10s 6d. Among the correspondence preserved at the museum is a letter with the printed heading 'W Howson Taylor, sole maker of Ruskin Pottery, Enamels, Buttons, Hat Pins and Brooches etc.' Edward Taylor's name may have disappeared from the stationery, but his presence was still as important as ever, in the area of design and promotion. The phrase 'sole maker of Ruskin Pottery' is also important, revealing as it does Howson Taylor's determination to protect his wares from predatory imitators. One such was Pascoe Tunnicliffe whose Ashby Potters Guild was set up at Woodville in Leicestershire in 1909. Tunnicliffe, an inspired glaze chemist who was a direct contemporary of Howson

Taylor, had connections with the Camm family of Smethwick, stained-glass makers and designers. Thomas Camm provided the shapes for the new Ashby venture, and there was also some contribution from his son Walter and daughter Florence, both of whom had been trained at Birmingham School of Art under Edward Taylor. With shapes and glazes very similar to Ruskin, and with an oval impressed back stamp closely modelled on the Ruskin mark, the Ashby Guild wares were too close for comfort. Even their literature paraphrased the introduction to the Taylors' 1905 catalogue stating:

'The colourings range from faint and slightly broken colours to the rich depths of enamel ... No attempt is made simply to reproduce old styles ... though several glazes similar to some of the Chinese of the best periods have been discovered and revived.'

The Taylors took prompt defensive action. they gave up the oval backstamp, they issued a new catalogue which omitted the introduction and, as described in the previous chapter, rationalised the range of shapes. They also made a new approach to John Ruskin's heir, Mrs Joan Ruskin Severn, for permission to formalise their use of the Ruskin name. This was accompanied by a crate of pottery, and it is this that probably persuaded Mrs Severn to grant the permission required. Her letter, written from Brantwood on 6th August 1909, gives clues to the types of wares in production at the time.

'Dear Sir,

We got back from the opening of the Ruskin Exhibition at Keswick yesterday evening too late to catch the post – or even unpack until this morning the pottery you have so kindly sent, as specimens of your work.

It has greatly impressed my husband and myself and we think it more than kind that you should wish us to accept as a gift, the specimens – some of which we greatly admire, and feel sure Mr Ruskin himself would also – especially those with the beautiful opalescent colouring and the more joyous blues, greens and golds, rather than the dull, sombre deep reds and browns.

There is an exquisite green bowl that every colour goes well with. We have tried red currants, grapes etc., and they all look lovely in it, and there is a vase of the same into which I have put my best roses, pink and deep red. It now stands in Ruskin's Study, in front of his portrait, and I feel we can now, gladly, give you permission to patent his name for your pottery.

The opalescent golden yellow bowls with wreathes of green leaves round are very lovely and delicate – and so light to hold in the hand.

The coppery one, though so rich, looks almost as if it were metal. The turquoise candle-sticks are charming and stand solidly, though having no rim, will need glasses – I am not sure whether the little saucer is to hold the thing of same hue as our egg-cup, or extinguisher.

The deep blue lapis-lazuli blue is very fine – though I almost wish the inner side of the wreathed little bowl were blue also instead of purple.

Then even on the dark ones there is a wonderful bloom, almost like that on a ripe plum. The greyish vase is not so interesting in colour – though useful in form – but it is delightful the variety and unexpected colouring that comes in varied light.

Please send us your "coloured illustration" circular that we may show it here to friends who may wish to get some.

Believe me, dear Sir, faithfully yours,
(signed) Joan Ruskin Severn'

On 2nd November 1909 a Certificate of Registration, under the Trade Marks Act 1905, of the Ruskin Pottery trade mark was issued to 'Mr William Howson Taylor and Mr Edward Richard Taylor trading as W Howson Taylor'.

Expanding production made increasing demands on the staff and so in 1909 an assistant firer, Albert Stephens, was recruited. The following year the paintress Annie Fletcher joined the pottery. Revealing is a surviving list of retailers from this time, which shows that Ruskin pottery was available nationwide. A total of 168 retailers is listed, ranging from major stores such as Liberty's, Goode's, Mortlock's, Kendall Milne and W H Smith to what are clearly small town craft shops. The list also indicates that Ruskin pottery could be obtained in the United States, Canada, New Zealand, Australia, South Africa, India and on the Continent.

There were more exhibitions in 1910. February saw the opening of the Arts and Crafts Exhibition Society's 9th show, with a good display of wares by 'W Howson Taylor and E R Taylor'. From the catalogue it is not possible to establish exactly what was shown, but prices ranged from 6d to £10. In April the Taylors entered their work in the International Competition in Artistic Pottery, but the results do not seem to be recorded. They also took part again in the Ideal Home Exhibition. The *Pottery Gazette* commented in

RUSKIN POTTERY.

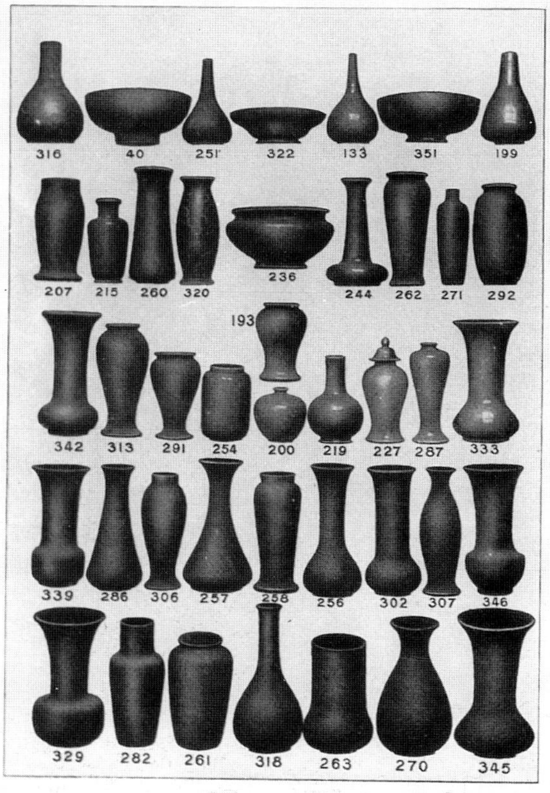

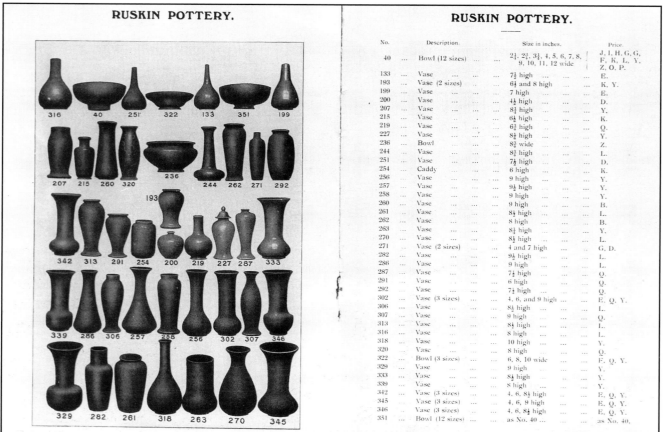

RUSKIN POTTERY.

No.	Description.	Size in inches.	Price.
40	Bowl (12 sizes)	2¼, 2¾, 3¼, 4, 5, 6, 7, 8, 9, 10, 11, 12 wide	J, I, H, G, G, F, K, L, Y, Z, O, P.
133	Vase	7½ high	E.
193	Vase (2 sizes)	6½ and 8 high	K, Y.
199	Vase	7 high	E.
200	Vase	4½ high	D.
207	Vase	8¼ high	Y.
215	Vase	6½ high	K.
219	Vase	6¾ high	Q.
227	Vase	8¼ high	Y.
236	Bowl	8¾ wide	Z.
244	Vase	8¾ high	L.
251	Vase	7½ high	D.
254	Caddy	6 high	K.
256	Vase	9 high	Y.
257	Vase	9½ high	Y.
258	Vase	9 high	Y.
260	Vase	9 high	B.
261	Vase	8½ high	L.
262	Vase	8 high	B.
263	Vase	8¼ high	Y.
270	Vase	8½ high	L.
271	Vase (2 sizes)	4 and 7 high	G, D.
282	Vase	9½ high	L.
286	Vase	9 high	L.
287	Vase	7½ high	Q.
291	Vase	6 high	Q.
292	Vase	7½ high	Q.
302	Vase (3 sizes)	4, 6, and 9 high	E, Q, Y.
306	Vase	8½ high	L.
307	Vase	9 high	Q.
313	Vase	8½ high	L.
316	Vase	8 high	L.
318	Vase	10 high	Y.
320	Vase	8 high	Q.
322	Bowl (3 sizes)	6, 8, 10 wide	E, Q, Y.
329	Vase	9 high	Y.
333	Vase	8½ high	Y.
339	Vase	8 high	Y.
342	Vase (3 sizes)	4, 6, 8½ high	E, Q, Y.
345	Vase (3 sizes)	4, 6, 9 high	E, Q, Y.
346	Vase (3 sizes)	4, 6, 8½ high	E, Q, Y.
351	Bowl (12 sizes)	as No. 40	as No. 40.

Above left: Howson Taylor in the pottery yard, about 1910. Above right: Certificate of Registration of the Ruskin Pottery trademark, issued 2nd November 1909. Below: Two of the eight pages in the 1909 catalogue of shapes.

RUSKIN POTTERY

(COLOURED GLAZES AND LUSTRES).

Highest Awards: GRAND PRIZES, ST. LOUIS, 1904; MILAN, 1906; FRANCO-BRITISH, 1908; "HORS CONCOURS," NEW ZEALAND, 1907.

BUTTONS for Dresses, &c., are now in great demand.

For Particulars apply to the Sole Maker,

W. HOWSON TAYLOR, Ruskin Pottery, West Smethwick, Near BIRMINGHAM.

London Wholesale Agents: Messrs. JESSON, BIRKETT & CO., 27, Ely Place, Holborn Circus, E.C.

Advertisement published in the July 1909 issue of the Pottery Gazette.

May, 'The Arts and Crafts section included Howson Taylor's fine display of his hand-made Ruskin pottery, which has a high artistic value and is already in demand for museums and the collections of connoisseurs ...' As in the previous exhibition, there was a large display of Ruskin buttons. However, the key event of the year was the Brussels International Exhibition.

As ever, the *Pottery Gazette* was fulsome in its praise of the Ruskin display:

'Many visitors find their attention arrested by the artistic shapes and rich colouring of Mr Taylor's productions ... His work is evidently progressive, as he has never surpassed some of the effects which he now seems to command at will. The decorations are superb, ranging from slightly broken colours, with and without patterns, to sang-de-boeuf, snake green, peach bloom and other transmutation colourings. It is pleasing also to observe that he does not depend entirely upon his glazes, wonderful as they are, but he also bestows much care and attention on the ware to which they are applied. The result in many cases is a really remarkable thinness and delicacy and a grace of shape that would have been fully appreciated by the great Master in art whose name they bear. Mr Taylor also shows Ruskin enamels used as insertions in jewellery, metalwork and furniture; and, in a case in the clothing section, Ruskin enamel buttons for dresses, sleeve-links, and hat pins, brooches, pendants, waist buckles, buttons &c. of Ruskin enamel mounted in silver ... Several pieces have been bought for museums and art galleries, and others find destinations in Egypt, the United States and various European countries.'

On 14th August, shortly after this report was published, the British stand at the Exhibition was destroyed by fire. The majority of the Ruskin pieces were lost, along with displays by other important British potters such as Bernard Moore. The losses sustained by the many British exhibitors taking part were considerable, with many displays uninsured. Howson Taylor estimated his loss at over £500, but was quick to despatch a new group of wares to Brussels to replace those destroyed. Ten of these, apparently all high fired flambé, were illustrated in the November edition of the *Pottery Gazette*. Despite the disaster, Howson Taylor was awarded two Grand Prix by the jury, which must have offered some consolation.

A further Grand Prix was gained at Turin the following year for a Ruskin display that again inspired the critics. In July the *Pottery Gazette* commented,

'Some of the finest glazes Mr Taylor has yet produced are applied to bowls of almost egg-shell thinness, the fine quality of the body being a feature of this ware. The orange-yellow lustre bowl seemed still to hold within its glaze a recollection of the living flame though which it had passed. Another had its fiery hue set off by a tender green shamrock pattern. A delicate pierced bowl and bright orange loving cup decorated with a twining vine call also for special mention.'

It is apparent from reports such as this that the lustre glazes were becoming as important as the high fired flambés. Also in 1911 was a London exhibition at the Crystal Palace, and the display here may have inspired a major article on modern pottery by H M Pemberton published in the *Art Journal*, which included three illustrations of 22 Ruskin pieces, with the emphasis on flambé pieces but with some soufflés and lustres. Indeed, lustres survive in greater numbers from this period, predominantly in the yellow and

Above: A display of wares sent out to the Brussels Exhibition to replace those lost in the fire, as published in the November 1910 issue of the Pottery Gazette.
Below: Group of wares illustrated in The Studio Yearbook for 1910.

orange ranges, but also in pink, mauve, kingfisher blue and bottle green, and their frequency suggests that they had already begun to replace the soufflé glazes in terms of popularity. At the same time, it is important to remember that lustres were more expensive, requiring an extra firing, and the higher prices may have deterred some buyers. Also, some of the colours, especially the yellows, tended to be rather impermanent. Another factor contributing to the relative scarcity today of early lustres could have been the thinness of the potting. While technically a sign of quality, this must have reduced the life expectancy of many items, particularly the bowls.

Early in 1911 Edward Taylor became ill, and on 14th January 1912 he died at Highfield Road, following an unsuccessful operation. The funeral took place four days later. A long obituary published in the

February issue of the *Pottery Gazette* left no room for doubt of the role played by Edward Taylor in establishing the success of the Ruskin Pottery:

> 'The efforts of the deceased for the last
> thirteen years to make pottery beautiful are
> now acknowledged, practically, throughout
> the world ... We leave others to speak of his
> abilities as an artist in oils – as an artist in
> ceramics his fame is assured.'

A similar sentiment was expressed some years later by the writer L B Powell, whose appreciation, *Howson Taylor – Master Potter* was published in 1936. Of Edward Taylor he wrote:

> 'He had lived long enough to see his pottery
> acknowledged in important places and by
> important people: had seen in the son, who
> now assumed complete control of the

business, the awakening of a genius which was to place Ruskin Pottery yet more securely among the finest pottery of any time.'

With no documentary evidence, it is impossible to judge the impact of his father's death upon Howson Taylor. Apart from the pottery, he had now to assume the responsibility for his mother and unmarried sisters. By the terms of Edward Taylor's will, written in March 1911, all of his estate was left in trust for his wife, much of it probably in the form of fixed income securities.

Far fewer pieces are known today in Britain bearing dates from 1911 to 1914 than from 1906 to 1910, but this cannot be taken to suggest a decline in production. It is more likely that increasing demands from export markets restricted domestic output. The relative shortage of information about this period also applies to the shapes, with a definite gap occurring in the factory's documented shape sequence. Only 12 of the 50 which followed on from the last catalogue, numbers 354 to 404, have been recorded. It has to be assumed that most of the others never went beyond the prototype, or experimental production stages. This pattern is consistent with previous catalogues where recorded examples never match all the illustrated shapes, and seems to confirm the view that the success, or failure, of shapes was determined by market response to the catalogue. The problem with these missing numbers is that there is, in this case, no catalogue, and yet some of them became well-known standards, for example the cylindrical vases 357, 358 and 402, the deep bowls 363 and 371, the elegant tall mei ping vase 366, first known in an example dated 1909, the ovoid vases 389, 390 and 399 and above all the ovoid caddy and cover, shape 362. This becomes the standard caddy from 1911, replacing all earlier designs, and was made in a range of sizes from miniatures less than an inch in height to over ten inches. It was also made as a pot pourri with the addition of perforated floral rosettes around the shoulder.

However, the British buyers were not completely ignored, and the Ruskin display at the Arts and Crafts Exhibition Society's 10th show, which opened at the Grafton Gallery, London, in November 1912, was bigger than ever. There were 54 vases, bowls, jars and caddies on show, at prices ranging from 3s 6d to £25. Indeed, the pieces priced at £2 and over account for over £123 out of a total value of £150, suggesting a change of policy since the Manchester exhibition of 1909 where the opposite had applied, and indicating that Howson Taylor was now relying increasingly on the expensive high fired flambé for his turnover. At the same time, it is likely that the price structure of important London exhibitions was higher than those held in the provinces. Such a change probably underlines Howson Taylor's emergence as the dominant power at the pottery since his father's death. In fact, it is possible to suggest that it was Edward Taylor who particularly favoured the soufflé glazes, which were gradually abandoned after his death. Commercial considerations may have played a part in the decision, but the switch to lustres and high fired flambés is characteristic of Howson Taylor's preference for demanding glaze technology, as well as a reflection of his sound business sense. In the end the soufflés, and in due course the lustres, were killed off by changes in fashion and cheap competition. Income derived from these higher priced sales may have given Howson Taylor the necessary financial strength to enable the pottery to survive the rigours of the First World War. Interestingly, in its review of the Taylor display at the Grafton Gallery exhibition, *The Studio* commented only on lustre glazes. Not recorded, inevitably, is how much Howson Taylor actually sold at an exhibition regarded by some critics as a financial failure.

On 14th January 1913, exactly a year after his father's death, Howson Taylor registered himself as sole proprietor of the Ruskin pottery trade mark. The same month, as though to underline his new authority, he issued a new catalogue, by far the most ambitious so far. With its hard binding, two colour plates, 30 black and white plates illustrating a wide range of shapes and glaze effects in elegant groups, and carefully constructed price scales related to the glaze finishes available, this document could hardly be a more fitting celebration of the achievement of the Taylor partnership, its productions and its crafts people. It confirms the trend in shape design established in the revised catalogues of 1906 and 1909, with an increasing emphasis being given to free interpretation of Chinese-style forms and detailing, perhaps a response to market demand. Certainly Chinese shapes, and Chinese porcelain, were strongly in vogue before the First World War. The range of shapes again becomes completely known from the illustrations in the 1913 catalogue, up to shape 440. Many fine new shapes appear but, as ever, only a few seem to have established themselves in the market place, judging by surviving examples, and some are completely unknown today apart from the catalogue illustration. Equally important is the catalogue's introduction, containing as it does Howson Taylor's personal design philosophy, and worth therefore quoting in full:

'Ruskin Pottery is named after the great writer and artist by special permission, and

LUSTRE GLAZES c1905-1926

Colour plates from 1920s publicity brochures; above: a range of lustre and other glazes, including yellow, orange, kingfisher, pink, mauve, green, and platinum foliate decoration, issued in 1925; below: the range of lustres shown in the 1924 Wembley Exhibition brochure, featuring new footed shapes and new mottled lustre effects.

Above: a display of tablewares featuring lustre glazes of the pre-war period and the 1920s, along with a few soufflé and matt glazes; below: colour plate from the 1913 catalogue showing lustre and soufflé glazes, including mauve (18L), yellow (15), orange (16) and kingfisher (2K). Colour 52 shows dove grey soufflé.

Top: range of lustre glazes of the pre- and post war periods, including kingfisher, orange, turquoise, dark green, delphinium blue, shell pink and yellow; above left: vase dated 1908 and caddy dated 1906, both with hare's fur crushed strawberry glaze, the vase additionally lustred with gold and purple to show the difference; above right: vase (shape 305) with fissured ice blue and sharp green lustres over yellow, oval mark and dated 1909; below: group of yellow lustre wares with painted foliate decoration, bowl 21 cm diameter, painted scissor mark and dated 1914.

Vase (shape 104) decorated with a kingfisher lustre glaze, 23 cm, impressed marks.

Above: two vases and a footed goblet with orange lustre glazes, larger vase 20 cm, impressed marks; below: group of vases with green and brown lustre glazes, left to right, green tea dust (shape 341) dated 1910, green tea dust (shape 302) dated 1920, mustard (shape 336) dated 1923, brown bronze, dated 1925, largest 24.5 cm.

Vases, pot pourris and other wares featuring lustre effects and piercing. Above: blue vase dated 1922, green vase with typical abraded effect, dated 1914, mottled yellow caddy dated 1924 and turquoise covered bowl dated 1921, larger vase 17.5 cm; below: blue caddy pot pourri, mottled yellow vase dated 1926, mottled footed vase and mottled covered caddy, dated 1920, vase 25.5 cm.

Four pieces showing pink lustres. Above left: vase (shape 271) with tortoiseshell effects, 25.4 cm, dated 1926; above right: vase (shape 264), 17 cm; below left: miniature caddy with unusual multicoloured effects and heart-shaped panels, 6.4 cm, dated 1911; below right: vase (shape 63) rose lustre overlaid with ice blue, 19.5 cm, dated 1923.

Above left: ogee stembowl with ochre and ice blue lustre effects over a hare's fur glaze, 18.8 cm, dated 1923; above right, apple green lustre vase (shape 12), 10 cm, dated 1923; below: wares featuring a mottled bronze glaze with brilliant mauve and green effects, bowl 25.5 cm diameter, dated 1923, powder bowl dated 1926.

its aims are good potting, beauty of form, and rich or tender colouring. Good potting means a sound body and delicate workmanship, and such a glaze as makes the ware as delightful to handle as to see. Some of the bowls are almost as light as egg-shell porcelain. The shapes are all made on the potter's wheel, and are such as grow out of the process under artistic guidance. The colourings range from slightly broken colours, through gradations of two colours, to textures and patternings rivalling cloisonné enamels and suggestive of the rich hues seen in rock pools at low tide; indeed, it was seeing these pools which gave the Ruskin potters the first inspiration as to what was desirable and might be possible in vitrified colours – delicate and brilliant colours made jewel-like by the medium through which they are seen. Each piece has a dominant note of broken colour, and these harmonize with home furnishings and costumes. No lead is used in making the glazes or colours, and all the patterns are hand-painted. No attempt is made to revive old styles, but trained art instincts and experience are brought to bear on the potter's usual materials, to see and to make artistic use of what experiments reveal.

Ruskin Pottery generally may be included in three groups:–

Group 1. – Soufflé Wares with and without hand-painted patterns. This group comprises a single colour note, or this varied slightly by mottlings, cloudings, or gradations of a harmonious colour. The colours range from dark blues and greens to turquoise and apple green, from purple to mauve and warm pink, and also greys and celadons. Many are enriched with hand-painted patterns adapted from plants unconventionalized except that they are painted in one flat colour and are kept subordinate.

Group 2. – Consists of a new treatment of lustres. The lemon-yellow and orange lustres with or without a green or bronze colour under-glaze pattern are quite new in methods and are specially beautiful products, as are also the Kingfisher blue and pearl blister lustres. Like the lustres of the best periods of ceramic art, they do not hide, but enhance the distinctive pottery character.

Group 3. – Real Flambé Ware, each piece being unique and unrepeatable. The colourings, textures and patternings of this real Flambé are as varied as is the number of individual pieces, and they include peach bloom, crushed strawberry, deep ruby, rouge Flambé (some of this last having green markings), ivory with pigeon's blood cloudings, purple-blue with turquoise cloudings, snake-green with ivory, grey, mauve or pigeon's blood diaperings, turquoise gradating to purple and with ruby veinings, dove-grey with diaperings, and ivory with grey diapers.

These wares differ entirely from the brilliant transparent red glaze pottery made for many years in Germany, America, etc., for these colours are generally obtained at a low heat, whereas the old Chinese Flambé, as also the Ruskin Flambé, have been submitted to the great heat of the potter's furnace which gives the full interpenetrative and palpitating colour effects – changes from splendour to splendour, or to pale tints which merge quite imperceptibly into the white of the body and the textures, veinings, and diapers, so characteristic of old Chinese.

Ruskin Pottery is made in vases and bowls in great variety, covered biscuit and jam jars, egg cups and stands, butter and sweet dishes, pot-pourri, plaques, loving cups, candlesticks, etc., also hat pins, sleeve links, buttons in great variety and of colours to match ladies' costumes, and enamels for insertion in jewellery, metal work and furniture.'

The status enjoyed by the Ruskin Pottery at home and abroad is also revealed in the catalogue, along with the interesting information that the ware had been shown at the Paris Salon:

'The Directors of Art Museums in England and abroad and private connoisseurs have purchased Ruskin Pottery for their collections. Their Majesties the King and Queen, and Queen Alexandra, Her Royal Highness Princess Louise, and other Members of the Royal Family of England have honoured this pottery by purchases, as have also artists, architects, and cultured people of all ranks and in most countries.'

The exhibitions of 1913 included an arts and crafts show at London's Grosvenor Gallery, and another appearance at the Ideal Home, with the

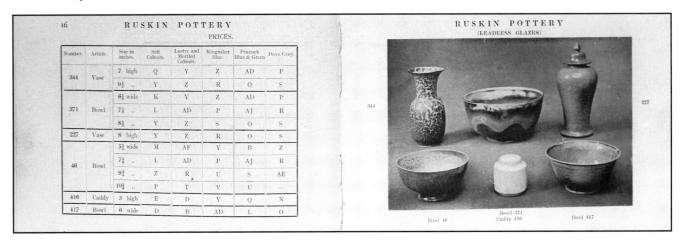

16 RUSKIN POTTERY

PRICES.

Number.	Article.	Size in inches.	Self Colours.	Lustre and Mottled Colours.	Kingfisher Blue.	Peacock Blue & Green	Dove Grey.
344	Vase	7 high	Q	Y	Z	AD	P
		9½ ,,	Y	Z	R	O	S
371	Bowl	6½ wide	K	Y	Z	AD	P
		7½ ,,	L	AD	P	AJ	R
		8½ ,,	Y	Z	S	O	S
227	Vase	8 high	Y	Z	R	O	S
46	Bowl	5¾ wide	M	AF	Y	B	Z
		7¾ ,,	L	AD	P	AJ	R
		9¾ ,,	Z	R	U	S	AE
		10¾ ,,	P	T	V	U	—
416	Caddy	3 high	E	D	Y	Q	N
417	Bowl	6 wide	D	B	AD	L	O

RUSKIN POTTERY
(LEADLESS GLAZES)

344 227

Bowl 46 Bowl 371 Caddy 416 Bowl 417

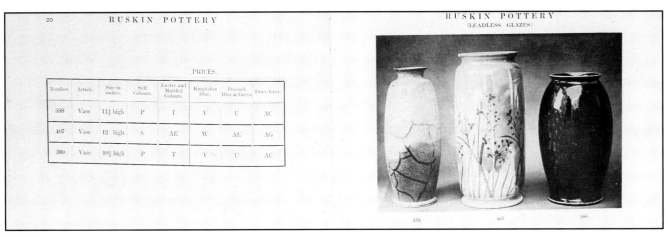

20 RUSKIN POTTERY

PRICES.

Number.	Article.	Size in inches.	Self Colours.	Lustre and Mottled Colours.	Kingfisher Blue.	Peacock Blue & Green	Dove Grey.
358	Vase	11½ high	P	T	V	U	AC
407	Vase	12 high	S	AE	W	AE	AG
389	Vase	10½ high	P	T	V	U	AC

RUSKIN POTTERY
(LEADLESS GLAZES)

358 407 389

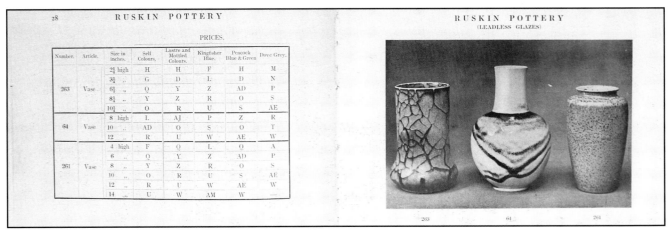

28 RUSKIN POTTERY

PRICES.

Number.	Article.	Size in inches.	Self Colours.	Lustre and Mottled Colours.	Kingfisher Blue.	Peacock Blue & Green	Dove Grey.
263	Vase	2¼ high	H	H	F	H	M
		3¼ ,,	G	D	L	D	N
		6¼ ,,	Q	Y	Z	AD	P
		8¼ ,,	Y	Z	R	O	S
		10¼ ,,	O	R	U	S	AE
64	Vase	8 high	L	AJ	P	Z	R
		10 ,,	AD	O	S	O	T
		12 ,,	R	U	W	AE	W
261	Vase	4 high	F	Q	L	Q	A
		6 ,,	Q	Y	Z	AD	P
		8 ,,	Y	Z	R	O	S
		10 ,,	O	R	U	S	AE
		12 ,,	R	U	W	AE	W
		14 ,,	U	W	AM	W	—

RUSKIN POTTERY
(LEADLESS GLAZES)

263 64 261

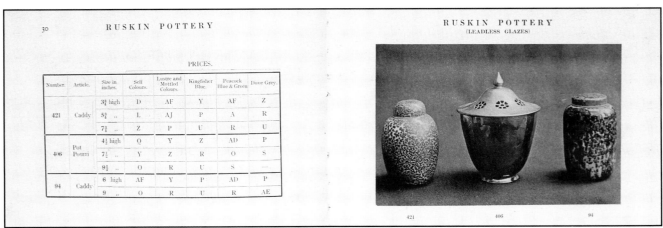

30 RUSKIN POTTERY

PRICES.

Number.	Article.	Size in inches.	Self Colours.	Lustre and Mottled Colours.	Kingfisher Blue.	Peacock Blue & Green	Dove Grey.
421	Caddy	3¾ high	D	AF	Y	AF	Z
		5¾ ,,	L	AJ	P	A	R
		7¾ ,,	Z	P	U	R	U
406	Pot Pourri	4½ high	Q	Y	Z	AD	P
		7½ ,,	Y	Z	R	O	S
		9½ ,,	O	R	U	S	—
94	Caddy	6 high	AF	Y	P	AD	P
		9 ,,	O	R	U	R	AE

RUSKIN POTTERY
(LEADLESS GLAZES)

421 406 94

Pages from the 1913 catalogue, showing shapes, sizes and price codes.

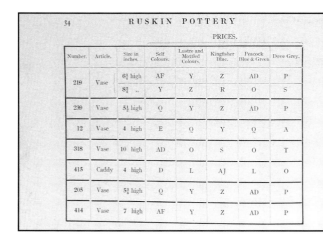

34 RUSKIN POTTERY
PRICES.

Number.	Article.	Size in inches.	Self Colours.	Lustre and Mottled Colours.	Kingfisher Blue.	Peacock Blue & Green	Dove Grey.
219	Vase	6¾ high	AF	Y	Z	AD	P
		8½ ..	Y	Z	R	O	S
239	Vase	5½ high	Q	Y	Z	AD	P
12	Vase	4 high	E	Q	Y	Q	A
318	Vase	10 high	AD	O	S	O	T
415	Caddy	4 high	D	L	AJ	L	O
205	Vase	5¾ high	Q	Y	Z	AD	P
414	Vase	7 high	AF	Y	Z	AD	P

RUSKIN POTTERY
(LEADLESS GLAZES)

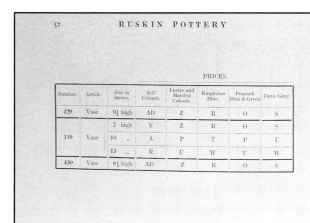

52 RUSKIN POTTERY

PRICES.

Number.	Article.	Size in inches.	Self Colours.	Lustre and Mottled Colours.	Kingfisher Blue.	Peacock Blue & Green	Dove Grey.
429	Vase	9¼ high	AD	Z	R	O	S
119	Vase	7 high	Y	Z	R	O	S
		10 ..	A	P	T	P	U
		13 ..	R	U	W	U	W
430	Vase	9¼ high	AD	Z	R	O	S

RUSKIN POTTERY
(LEADLESS GLAZES)

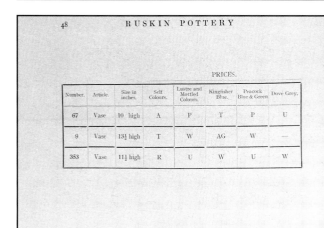

48 RUSKIN POTTERY

PRICES.

Number.	Article.	Size in inches.	Self Colours.	Lustre and Mottled Colours.	Kingfisher Blue.	Peacock Blue & Green	Dove Grey.
67	Vase	10 high	A	P	T	P	U
9	Vase	13½ high	T	W	AG	W	—
353	Vase	11½ high	R	U	W	U	W

RUSKIN POTTERY
(LEADLESS GLAZES)

66 RUSKIN POTTERY

PRICES.

Number.	Article.	Size in inches.	Self Colours.	Lustre and Mottled Colours.	Kingfisher Blue.	Peacock Blue & Green	Dove Grey.
440	Vase	4½ high	D	AF	Y	AF	Z
362	Pot Pourri	3 high	D	Q	Y	AF	A
		4½ ..	AF	L	Z	Y	O
		5½ ..	Y	Z	P	Z	S
		7 ..	O	P	S	R	U
		8½ ..	P	S	U	S	V
		10 ..	U	AL	W	AL	AM
242	Vase	4½ high	Q	L	AD	L	O

RUSKIN POTTERY
(LEADLESS GLAZES)

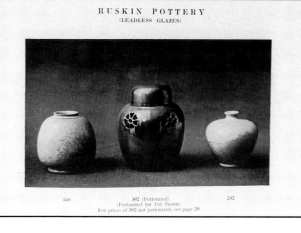

440   362 (Perforated)   242
(Perforated for Pot Pourri).
For prices of 362 not perforated, see page 26.

Pages from the 1913 catalogue, showing shapes, sizes and price codes.

pottery displayed, for some reason, 'at an Ironmongery stall'. However, far more important was yet another Grand Prix, awarded at the Exposition Universelle in Ghent, probably Howson Taylor's last major international prize. Once again the *Pottery Gazette* commented on:

> 'Mr Taylor's choice display of lustred bowls and vases of characteristic brilliance and fineness of body.'

There are also references to a pot with a 'quaker-like dove grey glaze', and to another sold to Copenhagen Museum. An interesting insight into the way such awards were celebrated at the pottery is offered by an article in the local paper, the *Smethwick Telephone*, published on 30th August 1913:

> 'It is customary for these achievements (Grand Prix awards) to be marked by the Principal (Mr W Howson Taylor) by an invitation to the whole of the work people to join in an excursion. This year's honour was celebrated by a circular tour, conducted by Messrs Cooks on Monday last. The Dukeries formed the centre for the day's enjoyment. The romantic and historical ground covered during the drive from Mansfield impressed all the visitors. The first halt was made at Welbeck Abbey, the forest home of the Duke of Portland and then the journey was continued through Sherwood Forest. In the course of the drive many other stately mansions were passed. The journey home from Mansfield was by saloon, and the opportunity was taken of congratulating Mr Howson Taylor and thanking him for his generous hospitality.'

From the slender evidence that survives from this period, it seems that lustre and the dove grey glaze were increasingly important elements in Ruskin production. However, from the point of view of the collector today the situation is far from clear-cut, for dove grey is virtually unknown. The glaze is illustrated in the 1913 catalogue and described as such, and so it is unlikely that it was never produced commercially. The catalogue contains a page listing the various types of glaze in production and these are presented in order of cost. First come the self-colours, that is to say the simpler soufflés, then the lustres, the mottled colours, the kingfisher blue lustre, the medium blue and finally the dove grey, 'priced as much again as lustre.' Dove grey was, therefore, extremely expensive, and this may have limited its appeal. There can be no doubt that Howson Taylor thought highly of it, but in this case he may have been out of touch with the market. Grey has never been very popular as a ceramic colour, and even the grey flambés were probably less interesting to the buying public. Some flambés are described as 'dove grey with diaperings' but these have to be seen as quite distinct from the dove grey soufflé. Successful, that is to say, richly coloured flambé could and did command high prices, and continues to do so today. The pale flambés have always been less attractive to collectors, and it is quite likely that they were simply seen as failures. High prices would, therefore, have made little sense in the market place.

Perhaps this is the place to consider the price of Ruskin pottery in relation to the contemporary cost of living. As has been shown from surviving exhibition price lists of the pre-war period, there was a steady move away from the cheaper soufflés towards the more expensive lustres and flambés. At Leeds in 1904 the total value of the Ruskin display was £25.11s.6d. By 1910 this had risen to £109.5s, of which the bulk was represented by the 19 pots priced between £2 and £10. Clearly, it was the expensive pieces that produced the profit. At the same time wages ranged from 32s per week for a craftsman to £20 a week for a senior professional man, with young professional men generally earning between £4 and £7 per week. The best high fired flambés and other pieces with exceptional glazes were priced from £1 to £15, and thus could only have been bought either by the very rich or the dedicated specialist collector. The market for Ruskin pottery was, therefore, very limited, and those who were prepared to pay the high prices were probably very selective. As a result, it is fair to say that very little dove grey was produced, and even less was sold.

Any study of the likely turnover of the factory during this period, bearing in mind the pricing and the number of staff involved, will reveal the importance of the export markets. From information gleaned by James Ruston from interviews with former employees, it is possible to estimate that the number of high fired flambés that could have been produced in any one year was probably about 250. With many of these costing the equivalent of a week's wages for a young professional man, the demand in Britain alone must have been too small to support the factory. Much of the output must have been going to the United States, and to other overseas markets.

It may well be that in this period Howson Taylor had, in any case, responded to market demand by cutting back on the high fired wares which were both expensive and potentially wasteful due to the high risk of failure. However, there is no doubt that the high fired wares were still in demand, and the groups of pots illustrated in *The Studio* yearbooks for 1909 and 1910 all have flambé glazes. It is also possible that he felt at this time that he had developed the flambés as far as he could. That the export trade dominated the market is made clear by an article in the edition of *The Connoisseur* published in April 1913 to commemorate the royal visit to the Potteries. Lamenting the lack of support offered to modern potters by English buyers and connoisseurs, the writer comments as follows:

> 'Modern English ceramic ware does not receive a tithe of the attention it deserves from the collector. He utilizes it for his household requirements, but does not introduce it into his cabinet ... The English connoisseur's glance is too retrospective, he is apt to collect the artistic triumphs of every age but his own. The antiquary of the future when he seeks examples of English domestic china produced in the age of George V will have to seek them in the Fifth Avenue mansions of New York or the palaces of Oriental potentates. The same rule holds good with regard to the purely ornamental pieces ... One sees pieces which in their fine simplicity of form and the lustre, richness and superb colouration of their glazes approach, if not equal, some of the best examples of oriental art. For these we are told there is no demand. They are not ostentatious enough for the ordinary purchaser ... and the connoisseur to whom they should appeal seems obsessed with the idea that age is the most necessary attribute of beauty ... American millionaires, who are the largest and most prodigal buyers of anything that possesses striking and apparent excellence being the principal customers ...'

The only documented event of 1914 appears to be the success achieved by two of Howson Taylor's employees in the pottery turning competition organised by the Worshipful Company of Turners. William Nixon won first prize and was admitted as a Freeman of the Company on 18th June, and Andrew Forrester came second, winning a bronze medallion. Later the same year Nixon was also awarded the Freedom of the City of London. The prize-winning piece, a turned table vase, was apparently finished in dove grey soufflé, a flambé glaze presumably being considered too risky for so important a pot. Nixon's actual prize-winning vase does not seem to have survived, and the so-called replica from the 1920s, in the form of a giant scent bottle on stand with threaded lid, may well bear no relation to Nixon's original table vase.

A final footnote to this pre-war period on a more personal level is supplied by information about a major collection of Ruskin pottery, formerly owned by a lady who was living in Hall Green at the time of her death in 1989. She had a remarkable Ruskin collection which included 17 high fired flambés which covered the period 1903 to the 1920s, along with excellent soufflés, lustres and crystallines, as well as a bowl with silver mounts by A E Jones. Included were pieces illustrated in both the 1905 and 1913 catalogues. Apart from the Ruskin wares, the lady's main enthusiasm appeared to be for Goss commemoratives.

Although of extraordinary quality, the Ruskin flambés in her collection mostly were marred by imperfections such as firing cracks, glaze patching, and chips to rims and bases, all of which were indicative of kiln damage. Such pieces, while technically and artistically important, would have been unsaleable, and are likely, therefore, to have been retained at the factory by Howson Taylor, who was known to have been very sensitive about the selling of imperfect pieces. Certainly Taylor would never have allowed anyone else to remove such pieces from the factory, let alone give them to a friend, and so the collection may well have been assembled during Taylor's lifetime, and with his assistance.

Until 1912 Howson Taylor's elder brother Bernard was living at a farm near Knowle, five miles from Hall Green, and he then moved a few miles south to Lapworth. Perhaps on one of his visits to his brother, Taylor met the lady and struck up a friendship with her, seeing her over a period of time, and bringing on each occasion a fine, but unsaleable, Ruskin pot chosen from the factory shelves. Another, equally mysterious collection of first rate, but slightly flawed, Ruskin wares was recently discovered in Smethwick Hall Girls School when it closed. Although there was no documentary evidence about the formation of the collection the pieces must, for the reasons described above, have come directly from Howson Taylor. Perhaps the school's headmistress at the time was, like the lady from Hall Green, a friend of Howson Taylor. The Smethwick Hall School collection has been given to Wednesbury Museum.

Chapter VII
THE FIRST WORLD WAR

When Britain declared war on Germany on 4th August 1914 everyone expected a short conflict and a rapid return to normality. As a result, the war took some time to have a direct effect upon small industries such as the Ruskin Pottery. As the war dragged on through 1915 all Britain's reserves began to dwindle and so encouragement was given to manufacturers with a good record of export sales to boost foreign currency earnings. With its established overseas markets, the pottery was well placed to play its part and, once conscription was introduced, it was able to use its record as an exporter to the United States to gain deferment from military service for its male employees. For at least the first year of the war the home market also continued much as before, and in July 1915 the *Pottery Gazette* published a long article on the Ruskin Pottery aimed directly at the retail trade. This identifies a new London agent, Green Brothers of Hatton Garden, and then goes on to describe the ware in familiar terms, making the point that, while some pieces are exclusive and thus expensive, commercial production had made others more accessible:

> 'Mr Taylor has ... brought some really artistic conceptions within the reach of every class of people able to appreciate a pottery that is soulful.'

The writer then particularly recommends certain types and colours of ware as good sellers, 'relied upon not to stick on one's shelves', including 'Nos 16 and 16MD (orange effect); the No 75 green, a delicate matt effect; the 5L, a delightful tortoiseshell effect, everywhere appreciated as a real achievement; a lavender glaze, almost bordering upon and at least suggestive of mother-of-pearl; and the "kingfisher blue", a triumph of colouration.' What articles such as this reveal is that the Ruskin Pottery was suffering from the progressive collapse of the luxury trade in the home market. The effects of the war, combined with increased competition, was forcing Howson Taylor to reduce his prices. One of his main competitors was the Ashby Potters Guild. Thanks to successes at exhibitions such as the Panama-Pacific, held in San Francisco during the summer of 1915, where they won a Medal of Honour, they were able to develop the American market at the expense of the Ruskin Pottery. The wares they produced, with glazes actively promoted as opalescent, crystalline, Chinese and lustre, were clearly directly competitive. Other British potters jumping on this particular bandwagon because of problems in the home market as a result of the war included George Clews of Tunstall, Stoke-on-Trent, and the Derbyshire potters William Ault and Bretby. The *Pottery Gazette* in 1914 and 1915 reported on 'the commercialisation of crystalline and opalescent glazes, rouge flambé etc.' along with 'metallic opaline, ... and aventurine glazes', noting at the same time that 'the shapes are mostly Chinese-inspired, well-suited to the flowing glazes'. Glaze effects were also a feature of the Ruskin display at the British Industries Fair, their appearance in 1915 being the first of many at this prestigious annual trade show. The *Pottery Gazette*'s writer commented: 'It included lustred, mottled and transmutation glazes in a variety of colours of peculiar rich tones, and the fortuitous results of the firing of some of the crystalline and flame varieties were really delightful.' The same year saw a group of high fired flambé wares illustrated in *The Studio* Yearbook, with further groups being shown in 1916 and 1917. However, the accompanying comments were somewhat dismissive. In 1915 the wares were described as: 'too well known and appreciated to require any special descriptions here' while in 1916 the magazine's critic wrote: '... it relies mostly on its original colouring and texture for any artistic value it possesses.' 'Lustred and iridescent art wares' were also to the fore at the 1916 British Industries Fair. The continuing importance of the home market was underlined in 1916 by a new series of simple advertisements highlighting Ruskin's 'artistic shapes and colours'. The particular needs of the home market were also reflected by the increased manufacture of candlesticks, with a number of examples known today bearing 1914 and 1915 dates and the soufflé glazes of the period, production inspired perhaps by the wartime Restricted Lighting Order.

However, 1916 also brought the war sharply into focus for small companies such as Ruskin. Severe restrictions were imposed by the government on the production of all kinds of wares for the home market, there was the first hint of forthcoming shortages of equipment and materials, and conscription threatened to decimate the work force. Harry Hill, responsible for clay preparation and factory maintenance, had already volunteered for army service by this time, and Howson Taylor began the constant and unremitting battle to keep his other key employees out of the services. From March 1916 Taylor gave up the home

Above: Illustration of five flambé vases, from The Studio Yearbook for 1915. The accompanying notice stated: 'The "Ruskin" pottery of Mr. Howson Taylor is too well-known and appreciated to require any special description here …'
Centre: Five flambé vases, illustrated in The Studio Yearbook for 1916.
Below: Five flambé vases, with distinctive patterning, illustrated in The Studio Yearbook for 1917.

trade, committing his production to export markets for the duration of the war. Only buttons, which were made entirely by female labour, continued to be supplied to the domestic market. Despite all this, Howson Taylor took his customary stand at the Arts and Crafts Exhibition Society's 11th show, held at the Royal Academy in London in November 1916. There was a good range of vases and bowls on display, ranging in price from 7s 6d to £50, with this very high price attached to a flambé vase and stand, 'thrown only, not turned'. Somewhat surprisingly, there was another London Arts and Crafts Exhibition Society show the following year, held in the autumn at the Royal Academy, but this must have been an exceptional event as the Society's 12th show was not held until 1923. These wartime displays were, in any case, probably related more to flag-waving than actual selling, and it is noticeable that dated Ruskin pieces made between 1916 and 1919 are extremely rare in Britain, apart from lustres.

With very few soufflé wares and practically no wartime flambés being produced from 1916, it appears that Taylor was relying largely on the standard lustres. However, also known from this period are a variety of experimental or limited production lustre glazes, including dark red and bronze, maroon and tan and a silvery grey, along with a glossy ivory and tan glaze with pale blue crystalline formations. Also from the 1916 period are a very small number of vases with a matt black glaze, with decoration of grasses in silver. These unusual effects apart, lustre production seems to have followed the immediate pre-war pattern, with few new developments. All the more remarkable, therefore, are the elegant scent bottles with silver or ivory stoppers made in about 1918, and decorated with orange or turquoise lustre glazes. Such luxury items must have been made for export, for there can have been no demand for such expensive wares on the home market.

The strength of the Ruskin Pottery's export business was clearly considerable. Even without the home market, output was maintained, and Howson Taylor does not seem to have been tempted, like so many of his contemporaries, to tender for lucrative war department contracts. There are no Ruskin army mugs, inhalers or bedpans to interest and amuse collectors today. At the same time, Howson Taylor was looking ahead to the end of the war and the resumption of normal trading, and this probably encouraged him to produce a new publicity pamphlet, described by the *Pottery Gazette* on 2nd April, 1917 as 'a neat little booklet'. With its small size, green paper covers, six new colour plates and descriptive text covering the types of ware made and the glazes used,

this booklet marks a break with the lavishly illustrated shape catalogues of the pre-war period. Shown instead are two examples of flambé, two groups of mottled yellow and orange lustre, and two plates of coloured enamels, one with them mounted up as jewellery. War-time expediency may have inspired its production, but from now on Howson Taylor continued to rely on this type of promotional material. The 1917 booklet was to be the first of a range of deliberately ephemeral and easily updated brochures, leaflets and sets of postcards, simple vehicles that were to support the factory through the 1920s.

The pottery's most critical year proved to be 1918. The condition of plant, equipment and the buildings themselves was poor after several years without regular maintenance, and spare parts were virtually unobtainable. The clay preparation area was the worst, with all the machinery on its last legs. At the same time, Howson Taylor began to lose his battles with the recruiting agencies. His own exemption from military service remained, but one by one his staff were forced to join up. First to go was Andrew Forrester, who joined the Royal Air Force in 1918. By October both William Nixon and Jack Cooksey had been conscripted, leaving only William Forrester the thrower, Percy Holland the turner, Albert Stephens the assistant fireman and Ernest Porter the placer and fireman. Also present was Harry Boswell, a general handyman who had joined during the war. With this skeleton team Howson Taylor was able to keep going, but he knew that if he lost Forrester, production would have to stop. The true state of affairs is revealed by a series of letters sent by Howson Taylor to Harry Hill, which was carefully preserved by Hill's family. Taylor apparently wrote regularly to all his employees away on military service, and the sentiments expressed show him to have been an unusually caring man, genuinely missing the team spirit of the pre-war era at Oldbury Road. Excerpts from a number of letters written to Hill were included in James Ruston's book, but they are worth quoting again as they give a vital insight into Howson Taylor's character, and show him to be neither reserved nor unapproachable. On 11th August 1918 he wrote largely in practical terms, describing the state of the factory: 'When this war is over and you are back at work we shall want a new plant in the slip house as it is all tumbling to pieces, it is worn out.' By 10th October things had got much worse, and the letters became more personal:

'Percy is still O.K. Nixon is scrubbing floors, Jack cleaning wash basins and Andrew stoking gas plant. Uncle (William Forrester) is away with the 'flu and

METAL MOUNTED WARES

Ruskin enamels and jewels, in soufflé and flambé glazes, mounted as jewellery and into a copper salver, on a background of Taylor tiles.

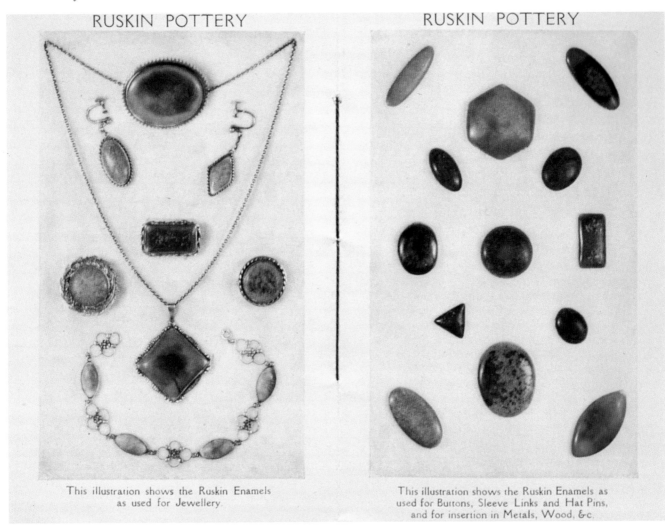

RUSKIN POTTERY

RUSKIN POTTERY

This illustration shows the Ruskin Enamels
as used for Jewellery.

This illustration shows the Ruskin Enamels as
used for Buttons, Sleeve Links and Hat Pins,
and for insertion in Metals, Wood, &c.

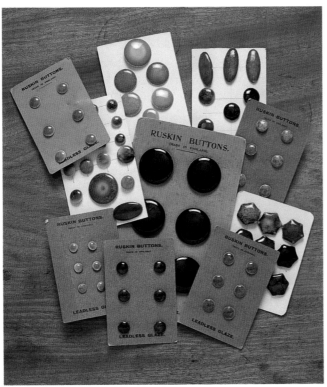

Above: colour plates from the 1917 publicity brochure, showing soufflé enamels; below left: a selection of carded buttons; below right: pewter salver by James Dixon of Sheffield inset with heart-shaped soufflé enamels, c1902 and a vase (shape 35) with blue-green soufflé glaze splashed with purple, 6.3 cm, impressed WHT monogram.

Display of enamels, roundels, buttons and other pieces for metal mounting with a variety of soufflé and flambé glaze effects, including two rectangular plaques with the 1908 'trickle' aventurine glaze.

Above: Ruskin wares mounted in silver by A. E. Jones, left, bowl with blue-green semi-matt glaze, the mounts inspired by an early 16th century piece presented to New College, Oxford, hallmarks for 1938, right, splashed flambé preserve jar with silver cover, hallmarks for 1920; below left: anodised copper coal box set with large soufflé glazed roundels, 41 cm; below right: anodised copper box set with 4 soufflé glazed enamels, perhaps made by Harry Handley, c1907.

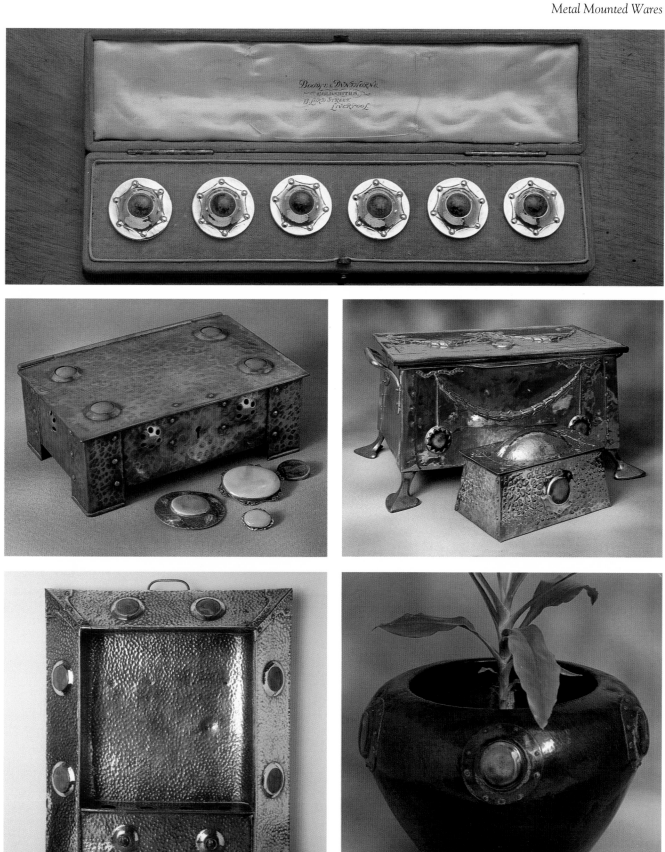

Range of wares mounted with soufflé glazed enamels and roundels; top: boxed set of silver buttons, 1908; above left: anodised copper jewel box and silver and pewter mounted jewellery; above right; anodised copper jewel caskets; below left: copper electric fire; below right: dark anodised copper plant pot; all about 1908.

THE FIRST WORLD WAR

Vase (shape 261) with a crushed strawberry soufflé glaze overlaid with darker tones, 31.5 cm, dated 1916.

Range of war-time production; top left: three lustres, a miniature pot pourri in purple and black peacock, 8.9 cm, dated 1917, turquoise scent bottle with ivory stopper, 12 cm, c1918, vase with brilliant silver grey glaze, 10 cm, dated 1917; top right: vase (shape 313) with blue-green soufflé glaze, 22.5 cm, dated 1915; centre: mottled flambé glazed vase with ivory ground, 21 cm, dated 1915; below left: mottled and smokey grey flambé glazed vase, 35.5 cm, dated 1916; below right: two matt black vases with silver foliate decoration, larger 16 cm, dated 1916.

DOVE GREY

Right: vase (shape 297) with a mottled dove grey flambé glaze, 24 cm, illustrated in the 1913 catalogue; below: caddy (shape 362) with a fissured and mottled dove grey flambé glaze, 28 cm, dated 1913.

Edie has just come back to work and now Ernest is about to have it, so you can tell how lonely we are. Anyhow we are just able to keep going.' Later the same month, Taylor wrote again: 'Nixon has been over on leave this weekend, he looks very well, and has very little to do only cleaning up, what a waste of good labour, when he might be turning bowls for Export ... Thank God I am not in it, there is a consolation to be Grade 3.' The same letter ended with a sincere plea: 'Well Harry I will close now and trust you will soon be with us again.'

Even the end of the war brought little immediate respite. In March 1919 Taylor was still writing to Hill, then serving with the Royal Engineers in Baghdad:

> 'I have tried again to get your discharge as Bert (Albert Stephens, the assistant fireman) has suddenly gone out of his mind and is now in the Asylum. Poor fellow, it does seem sad especially as he has 2 children. Annie is getting better after a bad attack of the flu. Alice Parry has got it now, so we have no painter. Beat (Tilley) has had it very badly. Hurry up Harry and get back and come to Clent with us all. It is snowing hard today and very cold so we are going sledging and then for a good tea. Goodbye Harry, I do so long to see you again after all these years of absence.'

Such sentiments indicate an unusual relationship between employer and employees. In the event, Hill was not released by the army until 19th March 1920.

As shown in the letters, the influenza epidemic of 1918 and 1919 was also taking its toll, with various male and female employees absent for long periods. The key employees were not discharged from the services until 1919 and 1920, and the influenza continued to rage. However, Howson Taylor was able to report that the factory held good stocks for the 1918 Christmas season, suggesting perhaps a shift in emphasis away from export selling once the war was over. The end of the war also saw the presentation by Howson Taylor of the first of the 20 years' service awards, with certificates being given in December 1918 to William Forrester and Ernest Porter.

The 1913 catalogue, the last major factory shape book, with the later promotional booklets: anti-clockwise, the 1917 booklet, the 1924 booklet, and the French version of the booklet issued in 1925.

From the very few examples of Ruskin pottery bearing a 1919 date mark that are known today, it would seem that the year was devoted to a slow return to normality. Gradually, as the employees were released back into civilian life, essential repairs to the factory and its plant were carried out. The influenza victims recovered and returned to work. Production was in any case seriously hindered by the sudden illness and death of Albert Stephens, following his attack of insanity. It was not until 1920 that the Ruskin Pottery could claim to have recovered fully from the effects of the First World War, but by then the market conditions had radically changed. In the immediate post-war period the situation for small manufacturers was probably as bad as it had been at any time since 1914. Prices were low, the home market was depressed, and export trade was made risky and potentially disastrous by the unpredictability of the exchange rates. After years of shortages it was hard to generate public interest in anything other than the essential material, and enthusiasm for the kind of expensive luxury represented by the Ruskin wares was almost non-existent. However, all was to change over the next few years as the pottery, having survived the strains and tribulations of the war, began to rebuild its former reputation and markets, at home and abroad.

Chapter VIII
RUSKIN IN THE 1920s

By 1920 the Ruskin Pottery was getting back to normal. All employees had returned from military service, and Howson Taylor had celebrated their safe return by sending each man to his tailor to have a suit made at his expense. He also raised the standard weekly wage at the factory to £4.10s, a remarkably generous increase from the pre-war rate of £1.12s, acts that underlined the close relationship he enjoyed with his staff. With the home market open again after years of wartime restrictions, this was also a period of expansion, and a number of new employees joined the pottery. During 1920/21 there were up to 17 men and women working at the factory, a level of employment higher than at any other time in the pottery's history. This was celebrated by the famous group photograph taken by Harry Hill in 1920, which shows eight male and eight female employees, with Howson Taylor half hidden at the back, managing to look both proprietorial and happy. The family atmosphere of the factory, frequently mentioned by the former employees and their relatives interviewed in the 1960s by James Ruston, is confirmed by photographs such as this, and emphasised by the family units within the group. Included are a father and son, William and Wilfred Forrester, a father and daughter, William and Violette Nixon, a husband and wife, Andrew and Beat (formerly Tilley) Forrester, and two pairs of sisters, Mabel and May Morris and Maud and Alice Payne. In addition, William and Andrew Forrester were uncle and nephew and Annie Fletcher married Harry Hill in 1920. This pattern of family involvement had been established earlier with the Tilley sisters and Emily and Harry Boswell, but it was in the post-war period that the Ruskin Pottery became truly a family business.

Howson Taylor's close involvement with his 'family' of employees extended far beyond the confines of the factory and the working day. A feature of life at the Ruskin Pottery was the famous factory outings. This tradition had been established well before the war, both as a means of celebrating important events such as the awards won at international exhibitions, and as part of the general enthusiasm for visiting the countryside. Several former employees had cherished memories of the regular Saturday outings, either walks in the country or visits to famous beauty spots and historic houses. These were generally taken by train or charabanc, and most of the employees seem to have been happy to give up

their time in this way. It is possible that Howson Taylor used these outings to draw inspiration from nature for his coloured glaze effects, but more important seems to have been the sense of family they generated. Favoured areas were the Severn Valley, Kinver Edge, the Wyre Forest and the Clent Hills, although the first outing, recalled by Ernest Porter in 1955, was to Sutton Park and Streetly, north east of Birmingham. Unmarried as he was and living with his elderly mother and aging sisters, Howson Taylor seems to have centred his life upon the pottery and its staff. He is known to have worked long and hard, spending most of his waking hours at the factory, and he never took a holiday. Certainly the demands of glaze preparation and the long and complicated firings of the kilns would have made this to some extent a necessity, but it is clear from Taylor's total involvement with his work that he really had no other life. Many of his employees seem to have shared his dedication and long hours were worked without complaint when the pressures of the work demanded it. As a benevolent employer, Taylor paid overtime, but money does not seem to have been a major issue with the key members of his work force. Most lived close to the pottery, and so coming in after hours or at weekends was always quite simple. The regular group outings, therefore, represented a vital area of relaxation for all involved, with an atmosphere of easy friendship evocatively captured by the few photographs that survive.

In 1920 production began to return to pre-war levels but there was a change of emphasis. Judging from wares known today, very little soufflé was being produced. The concentration was now clearly on the lustre glazes, with high fired flambés being produced when time, and kiln capacity, allowed. Output was still based upon the shape range established by the 1913 catalogue, along with the enamels, buttons and other small wares that were still important in the pottery's turnover. The lack of significant shape development up to the early 1920s maintained the pattern established since the death of Edward Taylor in 1912, and this does seem to confirm his role as an important designer of shapes. It was not until 1923 that there was a clear move away from this dependence upon the pre-war period, as far as shapes and glaze colours were concerned.

It was also in 1920 that the Ruskin Pottery returned to the exhibition circuit, in this case to what

Howson Taylor with his staff, photographed by Harry Hill in 1920. Back row: Harry Boswell, Beat Tilley, Jack Cooksey, Ernest Porter, Andrew Forrester, Taylor, Percy Holland, Wilfred Forrester, William Forrester, William Nixon; centre row: Maud Payne, Mable Morris, Annie Fletcher, Edie Tedd, Alice Payne; in front: May Morris, Violette Nixon.

was to be the first of a series of displays of 'modern crafts and manufactures' organised by the British Institute of Industrial Art. Held in Knightsbridge, London, from June to September, this exhibition included a 'collection of Ruskin Pottery designed and executed by W Howson Taylor'. Unfortunately the catalogue gives no indication of the types of wares shown or their pricing, but the *Pottery Gazette*'s report on the exhibition, published in their October issue, mentions 'a particularly good crackled-glaze jar'. Further exhibitions organised by the British Institute of Industrial Art were held regularly through the 1920s and early 1930s, and the Ruskin Pottery seems to have been represented at a number of them, including 1921, 1922, 1923, 1924 (held in Manchester) and 1933. It is perhaps significant that Taylor did not send his wares to the 1929 exhibition, which was entitled 'British Industrial Art for the Slender Purse'. From the Ruskin point of view, the most important of these exhibitions was that held in 1923. For a start, the catalogue is, for once, fully detailed, enabling the Ruskin pieces to be clearly identified and priced. Secondly, an interesting range of contemporary potteries also had their work on show, including old rivals such as Pilkington, along

with many of the new studio potters such as Bernard Leach, William Staite Murray, Reginald Wells, Dora Lunn, Katherine Pleydell Bouverie, Denise Wren and others. It was at this exhibition, held in London in September and October, that Taylor showed for the first time examples of a new range of glazes and shapes. The new glazes were combinations of colours, usually in streaked, mottled or hare's fur effects. Among those recorded are sharp green with pale yellow, sharp yellow with pale blue, sharp green with yellow and turquoise, mottled blue, yellow and lavender, ochre and blue, and bronze with mottled green and brown. Some were also used as soufflés, without the addition of lustre. These colours include some of the most spectacular effects that Howson Taylor ever achieved but production was limited by cost and so examples are rare today. In addition, many of these effects were produced only for a short time, until about 1926. Of the 28 pieces shown by Taylor in 1923, 14 were lustres. The majority were the standard colours, but two were certainly in the new mixed effects. There were also nine high fired flambés. As at exhibitions before and during the war, the flambés were the expensive pieces, and so it was these wares that must have been designed to generate the

Photographs taken on the famous weekend outings in the early 1920s. Above: Howson Taylor with a group of his employees, perhaps on Kinver Edge, left to right, Ernest Porter, William Nixon, Percy Holland, WHT, Jack Cooksey, William Forrester(?), Harry Boswell, Wilfred Forrester, Andrew Forrester.
Below: Getting ready for a char-a-banc tour. Standing: Andrew Forrester, Ernest Porter, Violette Nixon, Beat Tilley; seated: William Nixon, Ida Boswell, Mable Morris, Edie Tedd.

company's major income. The prices of all Ruskin wares were in line with their competitors but overall, given the inflation in general price levels during and after the war, they represent a decrease in real terms in comparison with pre-war ranges.

Also included in this 1923 exhibition were some of the new shapes, representing the first important change in style since 1913. This coordinated range featured a new series of shallow bowls, and related groups of dishes, cups and vases on stems, or hollow feet. Such ideas were not entirely new, for a few pieces on stemmed feet were included in the 1905 catalogue. What was new was the unity of the range as a whole – finely made, closely related shapes designed as vehicles for the new glaze effects. The inspiration was partly Chinese, with stem cups and the shallow bowls and dishes which come very close to the spirit of equivalent Chinese forms of the Yongzheng and Qianlong reigns of the Qing dynasty, themselves related to 14th- and 15th-century Yuan and Ming wares. Awareness of these earlier pieces is certainly suggested by the way Taylor consciously left some of his bases and footrims unglazed in oriental style. Harder to establish is the designer of this new range. A possible candidate is Wilfred Forrester, William's son, who joined the pottery as an apprentice at the end of 1919. An accomplished pianist with a degree in music, he may have been encouraged to bring a new style into the factory. Certainly by 1923 he would have been sufficiently experienced as a thrower to introduce an innovative style. Perhaps both he and Nixon's daughter Violette, working as a paintress since 1919, were seen by Taylor as the next generation in whose hands the future of the pottery lay. Harry Hill, writing to James Ruston, stated that after his wife Annie Fletcher left in 1921, no more painting was done. Although technically a paintress, Violette Nixon must, therefore, have been otherwise employed. It is unlikely that Howson Taylor himself was ever a designer of shapes, although clearly he had an important influence upon everything produced in his factory. In 1923 he was in his late forties and, presumably, thinking about the pottery's future and his possible successors. Encouraging young talent from among the closer members of his 'family' would have been the obvious route and certainly the design changes from the mid-1920s, with their echoes of contemporary Art Deco and Egyptiana, must have come from young minds receptive to contemporary styles.

This apart, Howson Taylor was notably unwilling to relinquish any control over the production process, and always insisted upon personal supervision of glaze preparation and firings. As a result the number of pots

that could be produced at any one time, particularly in the non-standard glazes, was determined by Taylor's availability. Over a long period, this affected patterns of production quite significantly. In 1907 output of high fired flambé fell because Taylor was fully occupied with developing the lustre glazes. When lustre was in full production he had to control the lustre firings himself, and so the output of flambés fell again. There was simply not enough time for him to do both at once. In 1912 all production dropped because Taylor was occupied with his father's death and the estate. The preparation of the new catalogue in 1913 also caused a noticeable drop in flambé output. In 1923, with the concentration on the new shapes and glazes, flambé production, judging by recorded pieces, was noticeably lower than in the immediately preceding and following years. The same thing happened in the late 1920s and early 1930s when the crystalline glazes were developed. No flambé wares are known at all dated 1930 and 1931, and very few for 1932, the peak years of crystalline production. When the flambés began again in 1933, the crystallines appear to have been greatly reduced. Despite his friendship with and, in many areas, his dependence upon, his workforce, it was Howson Taylor alone who could determine what the Ruskin Pottery actually produced, and when it made it. If he was busy with something else, such as lustres or crystallines, no flambé work was done, and if he was occupied with the flambés, not much else could happen. It was a highly personal, eccentric and, ultimately, inefficient way of working, but at least it did ensure that the wares made by Taylor at his Ruskin Pottery combined individuality with consistent high quality in a way that was beyond the reach of his more commercially minded rivals.

The appearance in 1923 of new shapes and glazes coincided with a new method of cataloguing and promoting the wares. In the past the pottery had relied on printed catalogues which illustrated every shape, with lists of sizes and glaze finishes available. Costly to produce and hard to amend, these had finished with the 1913 catalogue, the most extravagant of them all. Although shapes were altered to some extent between 1913 and 1923, the basic principle seems to have been a reliance upon those already available on the shelves, so to speak, and so no additional catalogues were issued. The only document issued by the pottery during this period seems to have been the 1917 booklet. With the new shape range coming onto the market in 1923, there was clearly a need for some form of catalogue that would both promote the wares and facilitate ordering by retailers. As usual with Ruskin, the range included

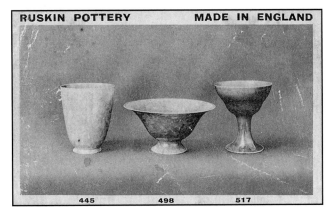

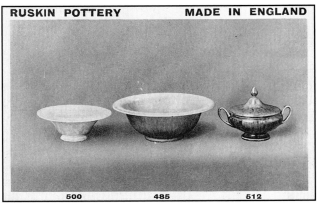

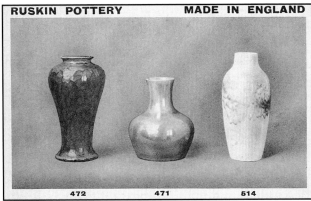

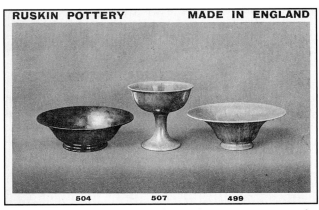

Part of the set of advertising cards issued in 1923 to promote the new shapes and glazes.

a number of variations on the main themes and so, rather than produce a formal catalogue in pre-war style, Taylor decided to issue a series of black and white postcards, each of which illustrated a group of the new shapes, identified by shape numbers, and presented in the style of the 1913 catalogue. These cards formed a cheap, selective and easily altered type of catalogue with considerable promotional potential. The 1913 catalogue listed shapes up to 440. However, the shape sequence shown by the cards is not entirely clear, for included on one postcard is shape 445. While this is only five shapes on from 1913, it is attached to a 1920s-style lustre beaker. Otherwise, the cards seem to show shapes from about 480 to at least 514, with the intervening 30 or so shapes presumably dating from 1918 to 1922. Only seven of these postcards have been recorded to date, and so it is not possible to say how many were included in the series. Judging from the range and variety of the new shapes there could have been at least 12 cards. It is also important to remember that not all the shapes shown on the cards were actually new. Included, for example, is shape 93 which dates back to the 1905 catalogue, one of a number of early shapes that enjoyed a new popularity in the 1920s. It is probably best to assume that the cards were issued to mark not just the new shapes, but also the new mottled lustre glaze effects, clearly visible even in black and white, which were used on a range of shapes old and new. The real problem, as ever with Ruskin, is the rarity today of actual examples that match the images on the cards. They must have been made, but few are known. Perhaps the thinness and delicacy of the potting, particularly on the rims, greatly reduced the likely survival rate. It is a pity, for those that do survive suggest that these wares could have represented one of Howson Taylor's greatest and most original achievements, in both technical and artistic terms.

A development of the new lustre ranges was the reappearance of tablewares. Finely potted tea and coffee sets were produced, probably, to judge by dated examples, from about 1926. Lustre colours used included the new ochre and blue, along with apple green, pink, delphinium and ice-blue. A few examples finished in the kingfisher lustre are also known. Plates were also made, along with low and high pedestal comports. Hairline cracking seems to have been a problem with the thinly made cups and so few sets seem to have survived intact. Seen as a whole, this late tableware was probably attractive but impractical, and expensive to make, and so it was discontinued in 1927, along with most of the lustre production. The only later tablewares recorded with matt or crystalline glazes are coffee pots, jugs, small bowls, sets of egg cups on a stand, and the lighthouse-shaped pepper and salt sets. These pieces, known also with soufflé, lustre and flambé glazes, were probably made over a considerable period, and so are in general terms hard to date precisely.

It is hard to measure the impact of the 1923 developments at the time, for few contemporary comments are known today. A large feature on Ruskin published in the January 1924 edition of the *Illustrated Country Review*, for example, concentrates on the flambés, relying for its information on the pre-war catalogue introductions. Equally general is an article on Howson Taylor in the March 1923 issue of *World's Work*, in the series Men and Women of Today. This does, however, confirm the Taylor method of working: 'He (WHT) strongly believes that personal supervision in every department is absolutely essential ...' At the same time it quotes a John Ruskin principle as the basis for the pottery's products, 'good craftsmanship and work of the fingers, joined with good emotion and work of the heart', and

then goes on to say that 'The workers ... are as happy in their work as their great patron would have desired them to be.' More valuable are references in the article to the strength of the American market, still the biggest buyer of Ruskin pottery. James Ruston refers to two orders for Marshall, Field & Company of Chicago, each for £5,000 worth of pottery. Assuming the figures to be correct, and knowing the production capacity of the kilns at this time, a £5,000 order could take up to six months to fulfill. While such orders were obviously beneficial, they must have caused serious production bottlenecks in all departments, and all other orders would inevitably have suffered. Apparently the orders were completed only through dedication, hard work and plenty of overtime. It is possible that much of the new lustre production went to North America, and so its rarity in Britain today could be a direct result of that. From the little evidence that survives, North America, India, the rest of the Colonial market, Japan, and parts of Europe, notably Germany, should all be richly endowed with Ruskin pottery.

The other important event of 1923 was the 12th display by the Arts and Crafts Exhibition Society, held at the Royal Academy in London. A small range of Ruskin wares was on show, credited to 'W Howson Taylor and Assistants'. It is possible that Taylor did not make a great effort with this show as he was already planning his display for a far more prestigious event, the British Empire Exhibition at Wembley. On 23rd April 1924 the exhibition was opened by King George V, and over the next few months over 17 million people passed through the turnstiles. Many of these must have seen the Ruskin stand, in the Palace of Industry, which included a full range of the pottery's products. The new shapes and glazes clearly featured prominently, catching the attention of the *Pottery Gazette*'s critic, who wrote in the July issue:

> 'We observed quite a number of new shapes, as well as new colour treatments. Particularly worthy of mention is a "Delphinium Blue" – a mottled blue of rare quality. Other distinctive colourings are mottled yellow, mahogany brown, and kingfisher blue. Many of the pieces are quite rightly spoken of as "unrepeatable" for Mr Howson Taylor is an artist as well as a potter, and he evidently produces many of his effects just for the very joy of producing something he has never produced before, and may never try to imitate again. The big variety of articles in which "Ruskin Pottery" is made is indicated by the exhibit, which includes vases and bowls, butter dishes,

The Ruskin display at the Paris Exhibition of 1925, illustrated in the Pottery Gazette, September 1925.

sweet dishes, loving cups, candlesticks, pot pourri jars, buttons and sleeve links.'

That Taylor regarded Wembley as an important exhibition is made clear by the publicity and display material that was made specially for the event. This included card mounts for brooches, but far more significant was the issue of a new factory booklet, presumably to coincide with the exhibition. The *Pottery Gazette* included a paragraph about the new booklet in its September 1924 issue. With its soft green cover the booklet followed the style established by the 1917 brochure. However, this one had a new format, tall and thin, and new colour plates, showing flambé and lustre glazes. The flambé group includes nine pieces, all based on shapes in the 1913 catalogue. Two were actually shown in the 1913 catalogue, and one other was illustrated in *The Studio Yearbook* in 1915. As a result, only two or, at most, three of the pieces in the colour plate were contemporary with the booklet. Taylor seems to have chosen them for their colouring and for the boldness of their surface effects, and generally speaking they represent a style and quality of Ruskin flambé almost unknown on the market today. The lustre group represents more typical factory production of the period. Six shapes come from the 1913 catalogue and three are from the new range. Of the lustres themselves, five are standard colours, yellow, pink, apple green, orange and ice-blue, all except the last named in production

at least since 1913, and four are the new, mottled effects, delphinium blue, brown and green, green and greys and blue and brown. The booklet's text is still largely that of the 1913 catalogue, but there is now no mention of soufflé glazes, or underglaze pattern painting. There were also changes in the type of ware listed. Gone are egg cups and stands, butter dishes, loving cups and hat pins, even though most of these were apparently shown at Wembley, and added are covered powder bowls, beakers and sports cups. Buttons, sleeve links and enamels for insertion in jewellery, metalwork and furniture were still an important part of the factory's output.

While the new lustres may have been dominant in commercial terms, it would be wrong to believe that they completely overshadowed the flambé glazes. Indeed, as indicated by the new booklet, experimental flambé was still very important. Coincidental with this period was the production of special enlarged versions of standard shapes, pieces designed to be rare and expensive vehicles on which the best glaze effects could be displayed. Included are onion and mallet-shaped vases with elongated necks, up to $14\frac{1}{2}$ inches in height, tall lily vases and large covered caddies. The largest known of these special pieces is a vase over 26 inches high. The majority were decorated with flambé effects, but some mottled lustres are known. The production period for these seems to have been from 1924 to 1926 and so they may have been made primarily for exhibition display. Certainly very small quantities of each were made, in some cases as few as seven or eight examples. Wembley may have been an ideal setting for such pieces but probably even more important in terms of Taylor's international reputation was the Ruskin display at the 1925 Paris Exposition des Arts Décoratifs. The range of flambé wares shown at Paris, curiously all standard 1913 shapes, can be seen in the photograph of the Ruskin display that appeared in the September 1925 edition of the *Pottery Gazette*. Accompanying the photograph was the following:

'Mr W Howson Taylor of West Smethwick is very strongly represented in the ceramic section. There are several separate displays of this manufacturer's productions, some of which strongly indicate his ability to produce artistic pottery of the chance or accidental type, while others portray more or less standardised effects in lustres and rich lustred colourings ... One is especially glad, therefore, to see "Ruskin Pottery" accorded such a prominent place in an exhibition that is concerned especially with industrial and decorative arts.'

FLAMBÉ WARES 1920-1927

Three examples of clouded red-purple flambé glazes on ivory grounds: vase, dated 1922, small caddy (shape 436), dated 1924, covered footed chalice, 30 cm, incised mark.

Left above: large vase (shape 261) with leopard skin mottled flambé glaze, 21 cm, dated 1926, vase (shape 304) with pared-effect blue and yellow flambé glaze, small vase (shape 328) with blue speckled flambé glaze, dated 1922; left below: three of the famous large mallet-shaped vases with contrasting flambé glazes, 36.5 cm, all dated 1924. Right above: large vases showing the rich flambé effects of the 1920s, left, 46.5 cm, dated 1925, centre, 31 cm, dated 1926, right, 40.5 cm, dated 1926; right below: vases with special flambé effects, left, striated blue-grey over liver red, 40.5 cm, dated 1922, centre, liver red splashed with pale blue, 22 cm, dated 1925, right, silver mounted, with blue and grey snakeskin glaze, 29 cm.

Top, far left: vase with mottled apple green flambé glaze, 23.5 cm, dated 1924; top, left: vase with ivory white ground speckled in green and black flambé, 24.5 cm, dated 1926; left, centre: colour plate from the 1925 publicity brochure, showing flambé glazed wares, 5 of which were shown in the 1913 catalogue and must date back at least to 1912; below, far left: famous red-green flambé caddy, shown in 1913 catalogue and 1925 publicity brochure, and always retained by Howson Taylor's wife; below left: footed vase and bowl (shape 495) with purple flecked turquoise flambé glaze, bowl dated 1924, vase 19 cm, dated 1927; above: vase in 1920's 'handmade' style with pronounced throwing rings, 36 cm, onion vase (shape 93), dated 1924.

Above left: vase (shape 282) with fugitive mottled flambé glaze, 40 cm, dated 1924; above right: mottled red flambé vase drilled to act as lampbase, 27 cm, dated 1920 (this vase was recorded in Howson Taylor's bedroom over a long period); below left: vase with mottled red-grey flambé glaze, 23 cm, dated 1925; below right: vase with mottled grey flambé glaze, 38.5 cm, dated 1926.

Above left: vase (shape 261) with streaky red-grey flambé glaze, 24 cm; above right: shallow bowl with mottled flambé glaze, 22.5 cm diameter, dated 1926; above centre: flambé eggshell bowl with pierced florets, 14.5 cm diameter, dated 1925; below; mottled and speckled red-purple flambé wares showing the continuity of the technique over a long period, vase, 24 cm, shown in The Studio Yearbook 1909, pot pourri and stand, dated 1927, square scent bottle with ivory stopper, 1930s.

Above: group of 1920s tablewares with flambé glazes, coffee pot, 18.5 cm, dated 1927; below: selection of miniature vases, caddies and a bowl, mostly in flambé glazes, and mostly dating from the 1920s and 1930s.

Three fine examples of flambé, mounted on matt black stands, illustrated in The Studio, November 1925.

In conjunction with the exhibition, Taylor published a new little brochure, in English and French versions, with new colour plates of flambé and lustre wares.

With the advantage of hindsight, it is ironical that few British potters, commercial or artistic, bothered to make an impact in Paris in an exhibition that was to change completely the nature of the decorative arts throughout the world. Gordon Forsyth, commenting on the British pottery at the exhibition, noted, 'a real lack of a spirit of adventure on the artistic side' and he was far from alone in this point of view. Three years after the event, in October 1928, *The Studio* commented, in a review of volumes publishing the exhibits of the various sections of the exhibition:

'The rare appearance of English productions is a reminder of the lamentable failure of this country to appreciate, at the time, the significance and importance of the Exhibition. Whether our failure was due ... to the apathy of English people and their strange indifference to activities in other countries, is a vexed question. The fact remains that comparatively few people troubled to cross the channel. Recently our designers and manufacturers have become vaguely conscious of the powerful impetus which the exhibition has given to progressive ideas in design and have found themselves compelled to revise their outlook, and respond, superficially at any rate to the new influences abroad.'

One of the main points of criticism was the dependence of British potters upon historical styles of oriental ceramics, and in particular the newly fashionable early stonewares of China. During the 1920s a number of potters joined Taylor in his exploration of high temperature flambé effects, including William Staite Murray, Reginald Wells and Charles Vyse. Taylor's response seems to have been an increased emphasis on the flambés, and the pursuit of high temperature effects that were not completely dependent upon Chinese sources. Scale, as mentioned above, became increasingly important. There is no doubt that Taylor considered that his flambés were moving in a new direction at this time, for he launched in 1925 an advertising campaign in *The Studio* to promote the 'New High Temperature Flambé Ware'. At the same time, three typical examples, large vases with dramatic flambé effects, were shown in the advertisement, mounted, unusually, on matt black Ruskin stands, made of plaster. These in themselves underline the change of direction. The use of stands in the Chinese style was a well-developed Ruskin habit. The 1905 catalogue includes many pieces shown on hardwood stands, and exhibition pieces were frequently displayed in this manner. The earliest recorded Ruskin ceramic stand dates from 1912, and from then on ceramic stands,

GEEHRTE DAME,
GEEHRTER HERR,

Vor allem bitte ich um Ihren Besuch meiner Ausstellung im ersten Stock.

Sie werden viel Schönes sehen. Kennen Sie die

RUSKIN = POTTERY

die unvergleichliche englische Kunst=Keramik? Die Ruskin=Töpferwaren sind, mit besonderer Erlaubnis, nach dem großen Schriftsteller und Kunstkritiker John Ruskin benannt worden. Diese Gefäße sind tadellos in Anlage und Material, von köstlicher Machart und besitzen eine Glasur, die es zu einem Vergnügen macht, die Waren anzuschauen und in der Hand zu halten. Einige Schalen sind fast so leicht wie Eierschalen=Porzellan. Solche Stücke machen Kennern Freude.

DER LADEN für GLAS & PORZELLAN

Weiss in der Streitgass

Denk stets daran

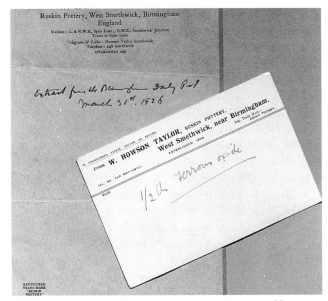

Above: Description of Ruskin Pottery included in a publicity brochure issued by a German china and glass shop in the 1920s
Below: Ruskin Pottery stationery of the 1920s

usually with flambé glazes, were associated with some important pieces. Notable was the vase and stand shown at the Arts and Crafts Exhibition Society's display in 1916, priced at £50. However, it is not certain the stand was ceramic. The 1925 matt black ones in *The Studio* may have been an experiment, but as none are known today they may not have been successful. The photograph of the pieces shown at

Paris in 1925 makes it clear that wooden stands were still being used at that date. However, from 1926 stands with flambé glazes are more common, and most dated examples known today were made in 1926 or 1927. The range of styles, shapes and sizes of ceramic stands is surprisingly large and, while many were made and glazed to match a particular pot and were probably sold with it, there are some that seem to be self-contained, to be used as required. Examples were also illustrated in *The Studio* Yearbooks for 1927, 1928 and 1929, along with four pieces on stands illustrated in *The Studio* itself in 1926. The one shown in the 1928 illustration was described as 'a carved pottery stand'. At the end of the 1920s a few stands were made with matt or crystalline glazes, mostly of the cast variety used with lampbases, but production of all stands seem to have finished by 1930. Perhaps the most characteristic of the Ruskin stands are those made in conjunction with the scent bottles with pagoda-shaped turned stoppers, made in 1926 and 1927. These, known in a number of sizes, are remarkable and finely engineered pieces, demanding great skill at every stage of production. With their complex shapes and fine finish, they may well represent the swansong of William Nixon, the head turner since 1901. In 1927 Nixon died, and no further scent bottles were made after that date.

Ruskin pottery was shown at a number of other exhibitions in 1925 and 1926. The first of a series of displays organised under the heading of The Applied Arts and Handicrafts Exhibition was held at the Royal Horticultural Hall, London in December 1924, with others following in June and December 1925 and June and December 1926. Taylor also showed his wares at an Artist Potters exhibition at Heal's, London in September 1925. However, it was 1926 that was to be particularly important, marking as it did Howson Taylor's 50th birthday. The year started with the 13th display by the Arts and Crafts Exhibition Society, held in London in January and February. Taylor showed five carefully selected and generally expensive flambé wares, ranging in price from £8 to £33. Dissatisfied with the manner of the display, in which the vases were shown individually along with objects by other makers and in other materials rather than as a group, Taylor resigned from the Society, despite pressure from W R Lethaby and Noel Rooke to change his mind. He was, in any case, probably feeling that in both style and cost his ceramics had moved away from the by now old-fashioned arts and crafts attitudes of the Society and its members. In April he showed at the British Industries Fair but not, as revealed in the *Pottery Gazette*, in the Ruskin name:

A GIFT TO THE BIRMINGHAM ART GALLERY.

OUR ILLUSTRATION SHOWS A COLLECTION OF RUSKIN POTTERY WHICH MR. W. HOWSON TAYLOR HAS PRE-SENTED TO THE BIRMINGHAM ART GALLERY IN MEMORY OF HIS FATHER, FORMERLY A HEADMASTER OF THE BIRMINGHAM MUNICIPAL SCHOOL OF ART. MR. HOWSON TAYLOR'S GRANDFATHER, MR. WILLIAM TAYLOR, WAS A POTTER IN BURSLEM.

Above: Four Ruskin potters, left to right, William Forrester, William Nixon, Ernest Porter, Jack Cooksey.
Below: The Birmingham Art Gallery Gift, illustrated in the Pottery Gazette May 1926.

'Mr W Howson Taylor ... had the advantage of the use by the firm of Albright & Wilson Ltd., at their stand in the Chemical Section, of a number of high-temperature flambé bowls and stands, which were utilised as containers for powdered chemicals. It was a charming collection of Mr Howson Taylor's best achievements, and, although not in the Pottery Section, the pieces thus displayed and put to such excellent use, excited a considerable measure of admiration.'

This unexpected display came about through the friendship between Taylor and A A King, a chemist with Albright & Wilson, and a source of advice for Taylor on the subject of ceramic chemistry, and it was repeated at the British Industries Fair the following year. Taylor celebrated his birthday by giving a collection of 35 examples of high temperature flambé to Birmingham Museum and Art Gallery 'in memory of his father'. Of the pieces in the gift, only four actually date from Edward Taylor's lifetime, with the majority having been made between 1920 and 1925. However, many of the shapes date back to the 1913 catalogue and constitute, therefore, a suitable celebration of his father's role in the development of the Ruskin Pottery. The glazes represent a comprehensive survey of Howson Taylor's achievement up to 1926. Along with excellent examples of red flambés, there are fine pieces illustrating the rare glaze effects to which Taylor gave descriptive names:

Shagreen, an ivory and green ground shaded with purple thickly flecked with dark green metallic spots
Robin's Egg, an ivory and pale green glaze shading to mauve and spotted and splashed with deep green
Snakeskin, a curdled and textured grey glaze shading to blue and parting in places to reveal small red patches on the buff body
Cloisonné, a mauve and pink glaze thickly spotted with metallic green and red
Peach bloom, an ivory glaze delicately shaded to peach and with deeper peach and pink clouding
Leopard's skin, a cream glaze shading to pale blue and mottled with pebbled areas of stone and buff edged in blue.

The May issue of the *Pottery Gazette* included a photograph of the gift, which was also widely reported in local newspapers.

Another celebration of Taylor's birthday took place in July when an exhibition of his wares was held at the Ruskin Gallery in Chamberlain Square, Birmingham, a new venture started by John Gibbins the previous year. The exhibition was previewed in the June 1926 issue of *The Studio*, with five flambé pieces illustrated:

'Mr Taylor tells us his chief aims are fine shapes, combined with delicate workmanship, rich and infinitely varied colouring, and a quality of surface that makes the ware as delightful to handle as to see.'

The year ended with a display at the Home Arts and Industries Exhibition, held in November at Drapers Hall, London. For the *Pottery Gazette*'s reporter, Taylor's exhibit was the best:

'Even a trade journalist is not immune from the covetous desire that Ruskin ware gives to all those who appreciate beautiful things.'

Chapter IX
THE FINAL YEARS

It can be argued that the Ruskin Pottery was at its peak in the early 1920s. Staffing levels reached a maximum in 1921, and then declined steadily through the rest of the decade, largely through natural wastage, with the result that by 1926 there were no more than ten employees. Notably reduced were the female staff. A pattern of significant change was underway from 1926, with 1927 seemingly the critical year. A number of factors underlines this, some forced on the factory by circumstances, and some reflecting a desire to move in new directions. A major event was the death of William Nixon in 1927. One of Taylor's closest friends among his staff, and someone who had played a vital role in maintaining the quality of Ruskin potting since 1901, Nixon was a great loss. Several significant Ruskin characteristics and techniques disappeared with him, notably the eggshell thinness of the turning, the pierced florets and several shape series, such as the ovoid caddies and the scent bottles on stands, along with the finely made footed wares. The use of dating seems to have temporarily stopped in 1928 and 1929, though this may not be connected with Nixon's death. A further blow was the death of the thrower Wilfred Forrester, at the early age of 31, a man who may well have been responsible for the new shapes of the early 1920s, along with Violette Nixon. In 1929 she left, and so from 1928 or 1929 Andrew Forrester must have played an increasingly creative role, thanks to his skills as a thrower, turner and, later, mould maker.

The impetus for change came also from the market place. By 1927 the demand for both the flambés and the lustred glazed wares was starting to fall. Such styles now seemed increasingly old-fashioned in the context of contemporary Art Deco modernism. At the same time, public taste had swung away from the sophisticated and complex oriental glazes towards the simpler styles of earlier periods. In the ascendant were the roughly made 'peasant' wares of studio potters such as Bernard Leach and Michael Cardew, with their inspiration drawn from the Chinese ceramics of the Song, Han and Tang dynasties, and from pre-industrial European country pottery. Taylor began to phase out his lustre production from 1927, a move echoed by contemporary lustre makers such as Moorcroft and Wedgwood, and the last known examples date from 1931.

Taylor's experiences in Paris in 1925 had also underlined the need for change. He must have been well aware of the old-fashioned Arts and Crafts styles of many of the British displays, and how unadventurous and traditional they had appeared beside the overt modernism of many European potters. At the same time, orientalism was clearly out, with inspiration now coming from sources as diverse as Africa and Russia. However, one of the most powerful of the many styles to be seen in Paris was that inspired by the discovery of the tomb of Tutankamen in 1922. Egyptiana was all the rage, and the classic styles of ancient Egypt were freely pillaged by designers and manufacturers in all areas of production. Readily available was a wealth of source material, in publications such as W M F Petrie's *The Arts and Crafts of Ancient Egypt*, issued in London in 1923. Taylor decided to join the Egyptian bandwagon, and from 1926 new shapes began to appear whose heavy, angular and thick-lipped silhouettes replaced the traditionally delicate Chinese curves. Wilfred Forrester and Violette Nixon are possible candidates for the new Egyptian ware designs. No catalogue is known for Ruskin's Egyptian ware, but some shapes are included on a single coloured sheet advertising the 'Art Craft' ware, or the A range, issued in 1927 or 1928. This, headed 'Matt, Semi-Matt and other Glazes', was accompanied by a price list for 15 pieces ranging from 1s. to 42s.6d, noting that 'all colours are the same price'. Examples from the A range were shown in *The Studio Yearbook* for 1928. Some pieces also appeared on a new series of coloured advertising postcards, probably issued in 1929. At least six were issued, showing varied groups of ware, including lamps, and priced on the back; a typical lamp was 48s.6d., complete. The cards also carry the following comments: 'They are made in matt, semi-matt and crystalline glazes. These colours are very effective and add beauty to the home.'

A feature of the new wares was their thick potting, along with the well-defined wreathing made by the potter's fingers during the throwing, qualities designed to match current enthusiasms for a hand-made look to the finish of 'artistic' pottery. Ironically, the fine, thin-walled finish that was a characteristic of William Nixon's turning was no longer seen as desirable, even if Nixon had still been alive and working. However, thick and heavy potting was not just a response to public taste, but was also a necessity for the new glazes that Taylor was developing at the same time. Despite having achieved an international

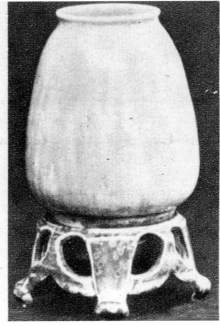

Above: The new shapes and glazes, illustrated in the Pottery Gazette, February 1928.
Below: Vases by the Ruskin Pottery. (1) High temperature sang de boeuf, with ivory-grey shoulder; (2) ivory glaze with brown markings on carved pottery stand; (3) fawn glaze with blue markings, from The Studio Yearbook for 1928.

reputation for his flambés and lustres, Taylor was still driven onwards by the need to conquer new fields, and from the mid-1920s his efforts were largely devoted to the successful production of crystalline and matt glazes. Such glazes take various forms. First are the so-called macro-crystallines, where the crystals in the glaze are large enough to be an element in the decoration. Next are the micro-crystallines, where the crystals are immersed in the matt, semi-matt or gloss glaze. Finally, there are the aventurines, really a sub-category of the micro group, where the

crystals are hidden in a deep brown glaze and are only visible in certain effects of light. The development of these complex and demanding glazes was a phenomenon of the 19th century, with many potters exploring the decorative potential of a high temperature technique whereby certain oxides, notably zinc, titanium, chrome and uranium, could be made to produce silicates to form crystals suspended in the glaze. The control of the process is critical, particularly during the cooling period. In addition, the glazes themselves are both very fluid, causing problems of adhesion to the surface of the pot, and very strong, causing the pot to crack or split apart. The difficulty of the process and the unpredictable nature of the results was a constant attraction to European potters. The first crystallines to be made in Europe were probably those produced successfully at Sèvres by Charles Lauth and Taxtile Doat from about 1880, with examples being exhibited in 1884. Doat continued to work in this field in France through the 1890s, and later in the United States. Similar experimental work was also carried out from 1886 in Copenhagen by Adolphe Clement and his successor V Engelhardt. Other potters working with crystalline glazes during this early period include Alexandre Bigot and Clement Massier in France, Brunnemann at Meissen, Wallender at Rorstrand and Hermann Seger at Berlin. Important work was also carried out in the United States from the mid-1880s at Rookwood, and later by Artus van Briggle, Charles Binns and Adelaide Alsop Robineau. The most spectacular effects were probably those achieved from 1909 at the University City Pottery, Missouri, initially by Mrs Robineau, Frederick Rhead and Taxtile Doat, and later by Doat alone. In most cases, development was brought to an end by the First World War.

The first successful producer of crystalline glazes in Britain was William Burton, whose experimental work from 1900 was first shown in public at Pilkington's Graves Gallery exhibition of 1904. Until about 1910 Burton's crystalline effects continued to be produced by Pilkington in a range of colours and styles. Bernard Moore also succeeded in producing crystalline glazes by 1904, and among the other British potters to explore this demanding process were the Ashby Potters Guild and Royal Doulton. However, production had largely ceased by 1914.

Howson Taylor's decision to produce crystallines in the mid-1920s is, therefore, rather surprising. He may have been inspired both by the need to make something new for the market, and by the challenge to succeed in a demanding field. In any case, he was not starting from scratch because some Ruskin glazes with crystalline effects had been produced as early as 1908, when a brown aventurine known in the factory as 'trickle' may have been shown at the Ideal Home Exhibition. During the war he had produced a silky ivory glaze with blue crystals, and it was this that seemed the starting point for a new series of crystalline effects that began to appear between 1924 and 1926. An extensive programme of glaze trials was carried out to create colours and textures suitable for the new Art Craft ware. In February 1928 the *Pottery Gazette* was able to report, in a lengthy article:

'It may be of interest to our readers to learn that, since June last, over 700 experiments have been made by Mr Howson Taylor, many of them on the basis of trial and error, and with a view to obtaining unique results.'

This article, with an illustration showing examples of the new styles and glazes, may well have been published to mark the launch onto the market of the new crystalline and matt effects. Certainly by this date the range was probably well developed, and included crystallines in shades of blue from lapis lazuli to ice, green, mostly jades, yellow and white, on predominantly ivory, mushroom, pale blue and jade grounds. A notable achievement was pots glazed with bands of contrasting colours, and with contrasting matt and gloss effects, developments that may well be unique to Ruskin, and which certainly put Howson Taylor's work apart from that produced by the crystalline pioneers of the turn of the century.

Taylor's experimental work at the end of the 1920s resulted in a remarkable variety of unusual glazes. Apart from the crystallines, there are the matt and semi-matt effects, usually in tones of blue, yellow and orange. Used on their own, or in combination, and applied precisely or with deliberate streaking effects, these are often startling or even garish in appearance. Linked were the gloss or soufflé glazes of the same period, often in deep and rich tones. The variations achieved by the blending of colours and technical effects were seemingly endless, and Taylor seems to have taken a delight in producing rare or even one-off glazes, with the result that categorisation is virtually impossible. Taylor himself clearly enjoyed this last chapter of his work, and was justly proud of the extraordinary results he achieved. Unfortunately, the lack of known contemporary critical comment makes it hard to judge their impact at the time, and since then collectors have tended to be rather dismissive of these late wares. Yet, at their best, they represent some of the most original, and the most complex of the pots that Taylor produced. In addition, they were a conscious attempt to stay in touch with the market. As the *Pottery Gazette* commented in 1928:

'Mr Howson Taylor is disposed to give the public what they want ...'

In the context of their time, Taylor's crystalline, matt and streaked effects do seem to have had a certain immediacy, and the blending of Art Deco shapes with matt and cool glazes was a style shared by potteries as diverse as Shelley, Wedgwood, Poole, Doulton, Pilkington and Bretby, to name but a few.

Also lacking from this period are records of Taylor's attendance at exhibitions, at home and

Above and below: 'Matt and Crystalline High Temperature Glazes', illustrated in the Pottery Gazette, February 1932.

period, and the late 1920s were marked by a flurry of general articles in magazines such as *Women's Pictorial, The Linen Press, The Country House and Estate, The Industrial World* and *The Furnishing Trades Organiser*. However, these were generally illustrated with standard and often already familiar pieces, and so can have done little to promote the new ranges.

More revealing is an article published in the *Birmingham Gazette* on 29th July 1930, in the series 'Romances of Midland Industries'. After describing the background and development of the pottery, the writer turns to current production:

'Up to about eight years ago lustre glazes were in great demand, but although there is still a certain sale for them, the modern generation prefers matt and crystalline glazes. The new production enables the pottery to be sold at a 25 to 30 per cent lower price than the lustred pieces, as it needs only two firings as against the five which many of the lustred pieces require. Everything round is made on the thrower's wheel, while other pieces have to be cast. In making these new matt glazes Mr. Howson Taylor carried out no less than 1,500 experiments to obtain new and delicate shades of colouring, with excellent results. Vases and bowls of great variety, covered biscuit and preserve jars, sweet dishes, pot pourri, plaques, finger bowls, candlesticks, powder bowls, tea wares and other articles are created in wonderful colours ... Each piece has a dominant note of broken colour, and these harmonise with home furnishings and costume.'

The article has two illustrations, one showing lamp bases being made, and the other loaded saggers being stacked in the kiln for firing.

Two developments may have prompted this move into the domestic market. First was the introduction, probably in 1929, of a range of moulded, or slip-cast, ware in contemporary geometric shapes. It has been said that this was an attempt to break into a cheaper market. However, equally important may have been the loss of certain key staff. The deaths of Nixon and Wilfred Forrester were followed, in 1929, by the departure of Nixon's daughter Violette, with the result that all production was now in the hands of William and Andrew Forrester, with the help of Percy Holland. It may well have become both impractical, and too expensive, to produce only thrown and turned ware, and so Andrew Forrester developed the moulded range, bringing the pottery, in the process, firmly up to date. However, it cannot have been

abroad. If anything, he seems to have deliberately ignored exhibitions between 1927 and the early 1930s, including both the regular domestic shows such as the British Industries Fair and the events organised by the British Institute of Industrial Art, along with the major international events such as the 1930 Antwerp exhibition. However, there is some evidence that he attended the European Arts and Crafts Fair held at Leipzig in 1929. Considering that so many new developments were taking place that, presumably, needed public exposure, it is surprising he attended so few exhibitions. However, shortage of money prompted by the increasing uncertainty in international markets could well have been a factor. Export-based industries producing luxury goods certainly suffered during the late 1920s and early 1930s. By contrast Taylor does seem to have made a bigger effort with the consumer press over the same

CRYSTALLINE AND OTHER LATE GLAZES
1922-1933

Matt and crystalline glaze effects, 1927-1933.

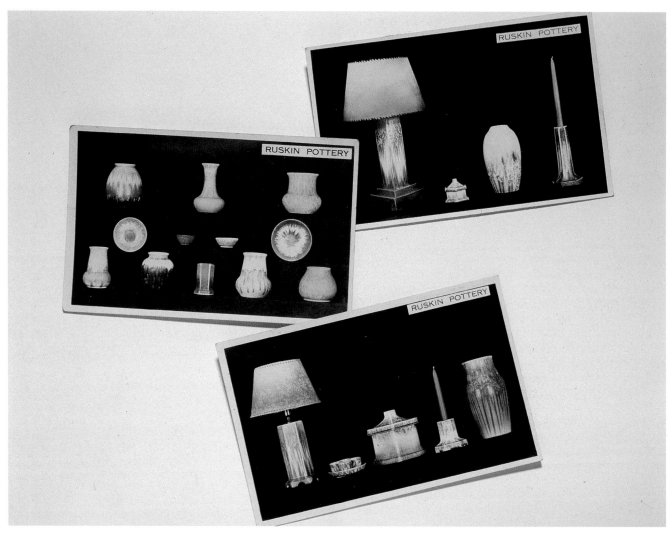

Above: advertising postcards from the series issued in about 1929 showing matt and crystalline glazes used on Art Craft and moulded wares; below: colour plate from the Art Craft 'A' Shape publicity folder, about 1928.

Above left: handled Egyptian ware vase (shape A20) with streaked and banded matt glazes, 25.5 cm; above right: jug with banded crystalline glazes, 21.5 cm, dated 1933; below: wares showing a range of banded matt and crystalline glaze effects, round vase (shape A6), 17.8 cm, dated 1930, impressed triangular mark and incised Taylor signature, moulded vase, 23.5 cm, dated 1930, vase (shape A21), 22.8 cm, dated 1931, impressed triangular mark and incised Taylor signature, covered jar, 17.8 cm, dated 1932.

Wares combining matt and gloss glazes, above left: vase (shape 261) 18 cm; above right, vase, 15 cm, dated 1927; below left: vase (shape 20), 20 cm, dated 1933; below right: vase (shape 258) 23 cm, dated 1932.

Above left: triangular section moulded lampbase on Art Deco foot with semi-matt and gloss glazes, 32 cm; above right: hexagonal moulded lampbase with banded semi-matt glazes, 19.5 cm; below: vase (shape 297) with mottled pale yellow crystalline glaze, 16.5 cm, and moulded footed bowl with yellow crystalline glaze on a glossy ivory ground, 14 cm diameter.

Vase (shape 297) with an ochre-blue soufflé glaze, 16.5 cm, dated 1930.

Wares with late mottled and monochrome glaze effects, above left: vase (shape A17) with marbled yellow matt glaze, 18 cm; above right: vase with mottled blue matt glaze, 22 cm; below left: vase (shape 344) with mottled red glaze perhaps imitating bakelite 23.5 cm, dated 1930; below right: vase (shape 271) with matt lava-like pale blue glaze breaking over a deep blue glossy ground, 25 cm.

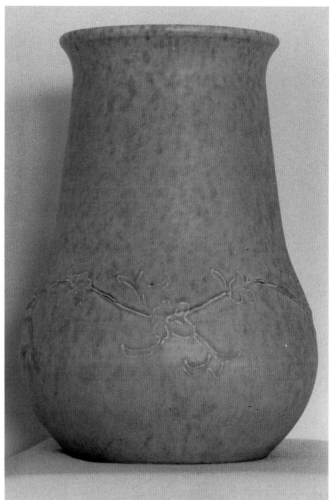

Above left: bowl (shape A4) with a crackled ash grey glaze in the style of Song dynasty wares, 16 cm diameter, dated 1927; above right: vase (shape A17) with matt glaze and slip-trailed and carved floral band, 28.5 cm; centre: paper-thin eggshell bowl (shape 40) with ivory patterning over an oatmeal ground, 18 cm diameter; right: vase with matt glaze and shallow spiral indents, 19 cm.

FLAMBÉ GLAZES 1927-1933

Vase and cover on stand in the form of a giant scent bottle, with a mottled grey-ivory flambé glaze with tones of pink and ochre, 36 cm, vase marked RUSKIN ENGLAND in green script in unglazed reserve, stand with impressed marks, dated 1927.

Above: wares with meandering floral bands moulded in relief, vase (shape A17) with an ivory speckled glaze, 27 cm, bowl (shape 40) with an ivory glaze with red detailing, pewter foot rim, 25 cm diameter; below: large vases from the late 1920s, in shapes introduced at that time, left, richly coloured red-green vase and stand, 44 cm, impressed marks, right, vase with mottled red-green glaze, 38 cm, dated 1932.

Above: a group of the characteristic pagoda-topped scent bottles of the later 1920s in a variety of flambé glazes, tallest 24.5 cm with stand, mostly dated 1926 or 1927; below: a group of carved stands in a range of styles and flambé glazes.

Above left: moulded wares with flambé glazes, a comport with hexagonal stem, 15.2 cm, and a lidded box, impressed marks; above right: a caddy with an unusual mottled peach bloom and ivory glaze, 17 cm, impressed marks; below left: large heavily potted vase and stand in studio style with a mottled glaze, 33 cm; below right, unusually shaped vase and stand with irregular red glazing splashed with green, 26 cm, impressed triangular mark and dated 1932.

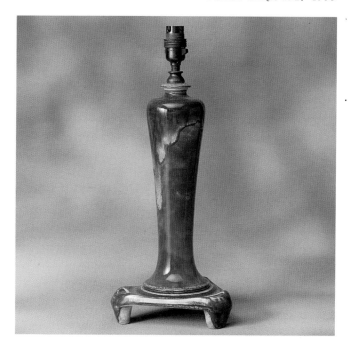

Right: flambé glazed vase (shape 336) adapted as a table lamp with tripod base and central brass fitting rod, 32.5 cm; below: three flambé glazed lamps showing different styles, left the standard caddy shape with attached cover and wooden base, 33.5 cm, centre, elongated vase with attached cover and central brass fitting rod, 31 cm, right, vase (shape 264) adapted with a pagoda-shaped base, 30 cm.

Above left: large vase with mottled flambé glaze showing uneven coverage of the foot, 38 cm, incised Howson Taylor signature, dated 1932; above right: lily vase (shape 63) and stand with mottled green-purple glaze, 34.5 cm, incised Howson Taylor signature, dated 1932; below: flambé glazed wares showing contrasting handle styles, left, globular vase with patchy, irregular glaze typical of the final year's production, 15.5 cm, dated 1933, right, richly coloured vase with anodised copper handles bolted on, 24 cm, oval mark, dated 1906.

Large flambé glazed vase with raised ribbing modelled in the clay, a style derived from the handled vases and jugs of the late period, 42 cm, dated 1932/3. The form of this vase is quite close to those made by the French potter Delaherche at the end of the 19th century.

Wares made early in the pottery's history and at the very end of production often showed a remarkable continuity of shape design and decoration. Above: two flambé glazed gourd-shaped vases, left, a purple-green mottled vase, 21 cm, impressed triangular mark, incised Howson Taylor signature, dated 1933, and a paper label in Nelly Taylor's writing stating 'out of the last kiln 1935', right, mottled blue vase (shape 201), 17 cm, dated 1906; below: vases (shape 89/263), left, with a moss green soufflé glaze, 21.5 cm, dated 1911, right, with a sang de boeuf glaze, 19.5 cm, dated 1933.

simple, quick or cheap to introduce slip-casting into a factory with no previous experience of the technique, and so both time and money would have been required. Nonetheless, the market demands for cheaper ware must have made these developments inevitable.

Apart from the geometric vases, bowls and covered boxes, it was the new range of table lamps that made the most of the moulding process. Lamps had occasionally been produced before the war, with the earliest recorded example being a flambé vase of 1905 adapted for electricity. Others are known from the 1912 to 1920 period, often with metal mounts, but the production of specially designed lamps on stands, as opposed to adapted vases, did not occur until the late 1920s. Then about 12 different shapes appeared, often very geometric in form, and most apparently designed for moulding, and for decoration with crystalline or matt glaze effects. Some flambé glazed examples are also known, but in general the high temperature glazes were associated more particularly with broader ovoid or cylindrical vase shapes. The new lamps, which were heavily advertised at the time, appear to have been sold with imitation vellum shades in suitable contemporary styles, echoing the conscious modernity of the advertisements themselves. Also introduced in about 1930 was a range of jugs, or rather, vases with handles, with a total of about ten shapes in production by 1933. Initially, these had matt and crystalline glazes, but from 1932 high fired flambé versions were also made.

The moulded wares do not seem to have been a great success in commercial terms. The geometry of the vases ranged from the conventional to the bizarre and, seen as a whole, the range seems to reflect a rather hasty flirtation with modernism that quickly went out of date. Certainly, examples are fairly rare today, suggesting a limited production. No dated examples have been recorded for 1932 or 1933, and so production probably ended in 1931, with a number of biscuit-fired pieces held in stock to satisfy any future demand. It is perhaps an irony that the last Ruskin wares to be illustrated in *The Studio Yearbook*, in 1930, were geometric table lamps, and Taylor can have derived no pleasure from the fact that he had become, in the eyes of *The Studio*, little more than a maker of light fittings. That *The Studio* no longer considered Ruskin a major pottery is underlined by the notable absence of the ware in an article on 'British Pottery of Today', published in the November 1931 issue. However, Taylor did take advertising space in the next issue, December 1931, listing vases, bowls and table lamps in matt, crystalline and *sang de*

DISTINCTIVE ELECTRIC TABLE LAMPS IN RUSKIN POTTERY

The three models illustrated are representative of a wide range of novel designs available in various colours, and in Matt, Semi-matt, Crystalline, and other glaze finishes. The shades, bound with thongs, are made of imitation vellum, coloured to harmonise with the pottery.

Photograph shows:
No. 4
Height of Pottery, 14 in.
Width of Shade, 10½ in.
No. 5
Height of Pottery, 12 in.
Width of Shade, 9 in.
No. 6
Height of Pottery, 12 in.
Width of Shade, 10½ in.
Further information gladly sent on request.

W. HOWSON TAYLOR
RUSKIN POTTERY   ::   WEST SMETHWICK

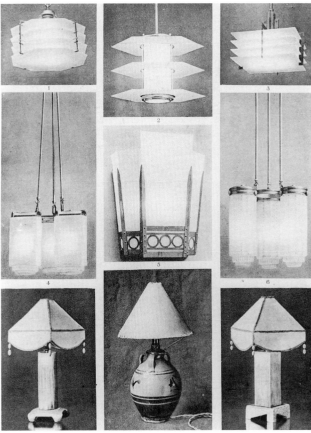

Above: Advertisement for Ruskin lamps, c1930.
Below: Electric light fittings illustrated in The Studio Yearbook for 1930, including Ruskin lamps in 'ivory and jade green' and 'green, blue and orange' matt crystalline glazes.

boeuf, along with 'Ruskin stones in all shapes and colours.' *The Studio*'s final gesture, in August 1933, was to omit any mention of Ruskin from an article on Pottery and Glassware in its 'Fine Craftsmanship' series, while showing a Ruskin crystalline vase on a glass table designed by Reco Capey, with a caption that ignored the vase completely.

While the emphasis was on the crystallines during this period, there was still considerable flambé production. Interestingly, this was also experimental, with many pieces from this period having features and effects previously unknown. Notable are new styles of

A series of photographs taken in 1930, possibly by the Birmingham Gazette, included these studies of, above, William Forrester throwing, below, Andrew Forrester turning and, right, Andrew Forrester applying handles.

piercing, wares with moulded decoration applied in relief, and a tonal range of ivory, greys and buffs, usually in splashed or mottled effects. These were achieved at the highest temperature range, and were a particular source of pride to Taylor, who, no doubt, priced them accordingly. However, there was a marked drop in flambé production between 1928 and 1933, with a concentration instead on the crystalline and matt glazes, with some late lustres, at least until 1931, in orange, apple green and crushed strawberry.

In 1930 the practice of date stamping the pots was resumed and a new style of marking was introduced, with the backstamp arranged as a triangle, composed of three elements, Ruskin, England and the date, said to indicate pieces turned by Percy Holland. Howson Taylor also began to incise his signature into the soft unfired ware, a curiously meaningless gesture as the style and finish of each signed piece would be unknown at that stage. As a result, his signature can be found on some surprisingly ordinary wares. Presumably this attempt at personalising the pots was inspired by the desire to give them greater market appeal. Perhaps he copied this habit from better-known rivals, such as Moorcroft, Clarice Cliff, Susie Cooper and Charlotte Rhead.

In 1933 the pottery seems to have experienced a kind of revolution. The emphasis switched back to flambé production, with two distinct styles of glaze

emerging from the kilns. The first was a spectacular bright red randomly scattered with patches of purple and green, a rich colour effect that was probably the most dramatic Taylor ever produced. This style had first appeared during the late 1920s. The second was far more restrained, an ivory ground with patchy red, liver or green clouding. Many of these late flambés reveal firing problems, with the glaze burning off in areas, and in others flowing down towards the base. As a result, bases had often to be ground down to remove the surplus glaze, something Taylor had not had to do since the very earliest years of production. It may be that these problems were caused by the switch from coal to gas firing, a change that had taken place in about 1932, perhaps both to save money and to make life easier for the fireman, Ernest Porter, by then in his sixties. Similar glaze flow problems can also be seen on many of the crystallines of this late period. For a number of reasons, Ruskin flambé wares bearing a 1933 date stamp do form a distinct group, with over 40 shapes represented. They stand apart from the rest of the pottery's production, but should not be seen in any way as inferior. The technical problems they reflect should be seen merely as another challenge that Howson Taylor enjoyed overcoming. At the same time, parallels between these late wares and some of the early flambés of 1904/5 suggest similar technical problems, perhaps

Vases with crystalline glazes, illustrated in the Pottery Gazette, July 1933, and showing the 'streaked effects, in colourings which form an integral part of the glaze...'

relating to difficulties with the control of firing temperatures, causing uneven, blotchy and liver-coloured reds on a greasy-looking ivory ground.

There was also a return to exhibitions, at home and abroad. In 1933 Taylor showed his wares at the International Exhibition of Decorative Arts in Milan, including vases, bowls and lamps in matt and crystalline glazes. Noted particularly were jade greens with milky variations of oranges, blues and yellows. At Dorland Hall in London in June and July, he took part in the Exhibition of British Industrial Art in Relation to the Home, showing 'a display of variously coloured wares' whose prices ranged from 1s to 18s. The July issue of the *Pottery Gazette* gives a good idea of the style of the display. Having referred to Mr Taylor as 'this chemist potter', a frequent term of address at this time, the writer went on:

> 'The pieces submitted ... consisted of vases, bowls and electric lamps. The shapes were characterised by their simplicity and uniqueness, and the colourings were for the most part shadings in various tones of blue, green, orange and similar reflective hues, intended to harmonise with either modern or antique furnishings.
>
> Streaked effects, in colourings which form an integral part of the glaze, and are, therefore, part and parcel of the pottery itself, are seen to a delightful effect in many of the modern "Ruskin" creations, which sound a high note in artistic pottery of the truly distinctive order.'

This pattern of renewed activity during the summer of 1933 suggests that the Ruskin pottery was enjoying a new lease of life. In fact, while these exhibitions were taking place, Howson Taylor was probably thinking about closing his pottery, and may have already decided to do so.

Chapter X
CLOSURE

On 20th December 1933 Howson Taylor formally announced the closure of the Ruskin Pottery. Although he gave his staff only one week's notice, he had obviously made the decision some time previously, for an article about the closure was published in the December issue of the *Pottery Gazette*. Appearing as it did at the beginning of the month, the issue must have been prepared for press in November. Details of the closure were also published in the Birmingham *Evening Despatch* on Wednesday 13th December, and in the *Birmingham Post* on 30th December. The former included details of Taylor's future plans:

> 'He intends to retire to the country, where he will be able to enter fully into the joys of gardening, a hobby which he dearly loves, and in which he has been unable to engage owing to his complete absorption in the art of pottery.'

Gardening also featured in the *Post's* longer article, but one of its more important themes was the possible loss to ceramics of Taylor's production secrets:

> 'The Ruskin Pottery has been produced by secret processes in firing and colouring to which Mr. Howson Taylor holds the key. It will be an unfortunate loss to industrial art if these secrets are not acquired by someone who will continue their development ... it would be a matter of profound regret if Mr. Howson Taylor's secrets, which had produced such beautiful results, were lost with him.'

In retrospect, Taylor's treatment of a loyal and devoted workforce seems rather cavalier, and uncharacteristic of a man well-known for his generosity towards his staff, particularly as those directly affected, Andrew Forrester, Harry Hill, Percy Holland, Ernest Porter and Beat Forrester (Tilley) had been with him at least since 1906. Porter, the fireman, had been with the Taylors continuously since the start of the pottery in 1898. Only two staff were retained to help with the closure and the disposal of stock, William Forrester and Jack Cooksey, and they remained as employees until the final closure in July 1935.

A number of features may have influenced Taylor's decision but, curiously, money does not seem to have been one of them. While trading conditions had not been particularly favourable since 1929, there is nothing to suggest that the pottery ever experienced financial problems. Production had continued normally right up to the end and as late as 1933 new shapes, notably the jug range, were being developed. Taylor's will, which showed a total of £10,916 duty paid, makes it clear that he was relatively well off and so money was not an issue. Making money had never, in any case, been a primary aim of the Taylors. At the same time, they do not seem to have lost much during the lifetime of the pottery.

More important were family matters. In November 1932 Taylor's elder brother Bernard had died, aged 59, killed by the same prostate disease that had ended Edward Taylor's life. Taylor himself may already have been ill, and perhaps was thinking that, in the light of the family's medical history, his own future was far from certain. Also important was the return in 1933 of Florence Tilley from the United States, with her son Harold C. Atherley, a move apparently encouraged by Taylor's impending retirement. On 10th January 1934 Howson Taylor and Florence Tilley were married at Birmingham Registry Office. Florence, the daughter of a mechanical engineer, was 51 at the time of the marriage. The marriage certificate records the couple as 'bachelor' and 'spinster' and so neither can have been married before.

It seems that as soon as he had closed the pottery Taylor began to put it out of commission, removing the heavy machinery and demolishing the kilns. A recurring theme, in newspaper reports and other documents, is his determination that no one else should ever be able to make Ruskin pottery, on the Oldbury Road site or anywhere else. A matter of importance for him was the disposal of the stock. The March 1934 issue of the *Pottery Gazette* carried the following advertisement:

> 'Ruskin Pottery ... customers desirous of purchasing specimens of Ruskin Pottery should do so now before all the stock is sold, as the sole maker, W. Howson Taylor, is retiring from business.'

Earlier that year, in January, there had been a selling exhibition at the Ruskin Gallery, Chamberlain Square, Birmingham, an event designed also to dispose of stock. A photograph of Howson Taylor with some of the display of predominantly flambé glazed pieces appeared in the *Evening Despatch* on

Above left: Howson Taylor at his exhibition at The Ruskin Gallery, Birmingham, in January 1934. Above right: Florence Taylor. Below: S Kaines Smith, the Keeper of the Birmingham Art Gallery, and a colleague with the special loan display of Ruskin wares in January 1934.

11th January. The accompanying article made it clear that Taylor had already decided not to release 'the secrets whereby his lovely glazes were created', the exhibition therefore giving collectors 'a final chance of obtaining some of the most exquisite pieces of an extinct ware'. The same month saw the opening at Birmingham Art Gallery of a special display of 14 pieces illustrative of the history of the Ruskin Pottery, loaned to the museum by Howson Taylor.

The next event was a formal celebration by the Borough of Smethwick of Taylor's contribution to the region, as an artist and as a model employer. This took the form of a resolution by the Smethwick Borough Council to:

'place on record their grateful acknowledgement of the valuable services rendered by him to the Borough and to the development of ceramic art over a great number of years, and to extend to him their best wishes for the enjoyment of health and happiness in his well-earned retirement.'

On 7th April 1934 the *Smethwick Telephone* reported the event in great detail, including the following remarks by Councillor Hadgkiss:

'... thousands of years hence archaeologists would be groping about in the dead and burned out mounds that they now knew as Smethwick and would come across pieces of Ruskin pottery and conclude that it was the only sign of civilisation, which would prove that the English were an artistic nation and Smethwick was the Athens of the post mediaeval age.'

The article also mentioned the gift by Taylor to the Borough of Smethwick some time earlier of some fine examples of his pottery. The publicity surrounding the closure of the pottery may have prompted the making of a photographic record of the factory by a member of the Smethwick Photographic Society. Now preserved in the Local Studies Archive of the Central Library, Smethwick, Warley, are 13 photographs including ones that show stages of production from the plant room to the showroom, via the kiln, the glaze spraying room and the biscuit warehouse, while others illustrate cases of flambé wares in Taylor's sitting room, and the pottery exterior. All are dated March 1934, and they were acquired by the library in July the same year, along with other, earlier photographs showing throwing, turning and handling by William and Andrew Forrester. The photograph of William Forrester had been published in the *Birmingham Gazette* in April 1930, along with some others presumably taken at the same time. The 1934 series is notable for the absence of staff, and for the amount of biscuit and uncompleted ware to be seen on the factory shelves.

Nothing further is known about Taylor's activities in 1934 until 21st December of that year, when a long interview with him was published in the *Birmingham Gazette*. This reveals a number of points of interest, including the fact that Mr & Mrs Taylor were soon to move to Devonshire. Despite a year's selling since the pottery's closure, the reporter noted that:

'...its shelves were crowded with his work. Blue vases, green bowls, red jugs – all aglitter with subtle golden shades, and so smooth and polished that you would have thought they were fashioned out of liquid.'

Even more important was the information it contained about Taylor's determination not to pass on his knowledge, a determination based on a promise made to his father never to reveal the secrets of his craft. Apparently Taylor had been offered large sums to sell his glaze and firing notes, by 'business men from London and New York' who had 'dangled thousands of pounds in front of him'. Other potters are also supposed to have tried to persuade him to sell, one of whom was reputed to have been William Moorcroft. However, this is unlikely, bearing in mind Moorcroft's personality and the financial state of his pottery at the time. Another approach is supposed to have come from Wengers, the glaze and ceramic equipment suppliers. Regardless of what offers and approaches Taylor may have received, he remained obdurate. As he told the *Gazette*'s reporter:

'I intend that my formulae and my secrets die with me. I think I am justified in deciding upon such a course. But don't let us talk of dying. I'm nearly 60, but I'm full of beans, and I intend to enjoy life. As soon as I have sold my stock, I am going to close the works. They will never be used for pottery again.'

This statement underlined the point made in the article's opening paragraph:

'Ruskin Pottery, West Smethwick, will soon be empty. Its last vase has been made; the fires of its ovens have been kindled for the last time...'

Taylor seems to have been as good as his word, for there are a number of reports of him and Florence spending long hours at the pottery burning notebooks, documents and records.

Interesting though it is, the article does not throw any light on the main question of this last period, namely whether Taylor used some of the remaining biscuit-fired stock to produce some final high fired flambé wares between the end of production in December 1933 and the early part of 1935. This controversy has been long debated, and the conflicting evidence suggests that it is unlikely ever to be satisfactorily resolved. It was the Ruskin enthusiast L B Powell who started the debate, stating in 1936 in his privately published memorial booklet, *Howson Taylor Master Potter*, the following:

'In the period – roughly a year – which followed the announcement of the closing of the factory, Howson Taylor coloured, glazed and fired a large number of pieces remaining in stock in biscuit form ... It is no secret among those who know him well that in this valedictory period some of the finest

Views of the Ruskin Pottery after its closure, from the series of photographs taken in March 1934. Above: finished ware in the showroom. Below: the glaze spraying area, with glazed wares ready for firing.

Above: Howson Taylor in the showroom. Below: the biscuit warehouse.

Finished ware in the showroom, from the March 1934 photographic series.

work was produced, and it was characteristic of him that, freed finally of all commercial considerations, he should devote to these pieces a more intensive degree of skill than ever before.'

Others have maintained this tradition. More evidence comes from a number of people who claim to have been present at the last kiln firing at the Ruskin Pottery. However, it seems impossible to establish a definite date for this event. One was Taylor's elder sister Nelly, who had apparently often attended the firing of the flambé kiln. By 1934 she was in her mid-60s, but little is known about her ceramic expertise. The main basis for her claim seems to be a vase, formerly in her possession, which has on its base a paper label stating, 'Out of the last kiln 1935'. Another was Harold Atherley, Florence's son. In a letter written in 1989, he stated:

> 'While on a visit to England I was there when they fired the last kiln before closing the works. I had the privilege of helping Mr Cooksey and Mr Forrester load the kiln. I didn't realise it then, but looking back I feel I participated in an historic event.'

Unfortunately, Mr Atherley did not mention the date of this event, but by implication it could have been after 1933 for Jack Cooksey and William Forrester would not otherwise have been undertaking tasks that would normally have been done by Ernest Porter.

A third was Robert Ferneyhough, a local boy and Ruskin enthusiast who had been befriended by Howson Taylor in the early 1930s, and who shared his love for the pottery. In due course Taylor's friendship with the boy led him not only to entrust him with a very considerable amount of unsold factory stock, but also to give him his personal collection of pieces that he had retained for one reason or another. These, mostly high fired flambé wares of remarkable quality, may have totalled several hundred pieces. The young Ferneyhough was also given the pottery letters that had graced the façade of the factory, now in the collection of Birmingham Museum and Art Gallery. At the time of this gift Robert Ferneyhough, who was born in November 1919, the son of James Alfred Ferneyhough, a house painter, and his wife Eunice Matilda, of Warley Road, Smethwick, was aged about 15. It seems that this unusual gift was confirmed as an official legacy after Taylor's death by Florence.

It would appear, therefore, that the last firing, whenever it occurred, was attended by Howson Taylor, his sister in her 60s, a young boy in his teens, an American in his late 20s and the two remaining employees, Cooksey and Forrester. Notably lacking apart from Taylor himself, and possibly Nelly, was anyone who actually knew how to fire a flambé kiln. Cooksey was the packer, retained to help dispose of the stock, while William Forrester, a thrower and one of the Taylor's first employees, was presumably still on the payroll largely for sentimental reasons. There was certainly no throwing to be done, although Forrester may have spent some of his time making the series of miniature vases and bowls produced at the end of the pottery's life.

The fireman, Ernest Porter, had left in December 1933. He lived very near the pottery and, when interviewed by James Ruston in the 1960s, he said that he had never been asked to help with any firings after 1933, and had not known of any taking place. Furthermore, he stated that no one else could have fired the kilns. This may not be entirely true, for the new gas-fired kiln may well have been simpler to operate, and may even have been installed for Taylor himself to use. Also interviewed at the same time was Florence Taylor, and she was adamant that no firings were carried out after 1933, on the grounds that her husband was by then a sick man incapable of undertaking any work other than that of running down the establishment. It is actually hard to believe that a man in his deteriorating physical condition could have prepared the glazes, glazed the pots, loaded the kiln, maintained the long and demanding firing cycle, unloaded the kiln and then ground off the surplus glaze characteristic of the late flambés without professional help. In December 1934, Taylor told the *Birmingham Gazette* that the kilns had been fired for the last time. He could have been firing during the latter part of 1934, but his wife denied it strongly. On 25th January 1935 he wrote to a friend, W V Turner:

> '... I have finished my work and ... nobody shall ever make Ruskin Pottery.'

Did Taylor change his mind and perhaps fire one last kiln early in January 1935, perhaps when Florence was away in Devon sorting out the new house? Or was Florence, for her own reasons, economical with the truth? There will probably always be uncertainty over the whole question of the late firings. The evidence is inconclusive either way and now, with all those involved dead, the debate is never likely to be resolved.

On 18th June 1935 Howson Taylor's mother Mary died, aged 97, and so Taylor finally inherited his share of what remained of his father's estate. In July the pottery, by now an empty shell, was closed for the last time, and Mr and Mrs Taylor, along with Harold Atherley, moved to their new house, Spring Bank, Ashprington, near Tuckenhay on the River Dart in Devonshire. Taylor was enthusiastic about his new life, and keen to get on with his garden, but his retirement was destined to be short-lived. On Sunday 22nd September 1935 William Howson Taylor died, killed by the same prostate disease that had ended both his father's and his brother's lives. He was buried in Ashprington churchyard, his grave marked by a rough-hewn block of Dartmoor granite.

Generous obituaries were published in the Birmingham *Evening Despatch*, the *Birmingham Daily Post*, the *Birmingham Mail* and the *Smethwick Telephone*, among others. Several included the following statement by Mr Kaines Smith, the keeper of the Birmingham Art Gallery:

> 'Quite apart from my personal liking for him, I regarded him as one of the greatest artist-craftsmen of our time. It is a terrible thing to think that his beautiful art is completely lost. He was a great artist and a most charming man.'

Another obituary appeared in the *Pottery Gazette* in November. Interestingly, this linked Taylor with his father:

> 'We deplore the passing of a potter of the attainments and calibre of Mr. W. Howson Taylor, and in paying this last tribute to his memory we would suggest that just as his father, the late Mr. Edward R Taylor, who

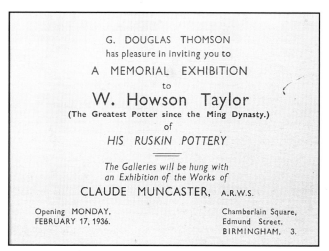

Invitation card for the Howson Taylor Memorial Exhibition, held at the Ruskin Gallery, Birmingham in February 1936.

was a former headmaster of the Birmingham School of Art, wielded a palpable influence for good in connection with general art matters in the Midlands, so Mr. W. Howson Taylor, his son, in the course of his pursuits as a chemist-artist-potter, has shed rays of sunshine through the pottery trimmings which he supplied to many a well-furnished home. Such men are rare and the sense of loss that they leave behind when they pass from amongst us is great indeed.'

On 17th February 1936 a memorial exhibition of Ruskin Pottery opened at the Ruskin Gallery in Chamberlain Square, Birmingham, organised by the gallery's new owner, G. Douglas Thomson. The exhibition's invitation card described Taylor as 'The Greatest Potter since the Ming Dynasty'. On view at the same time were paintings by Claude Muncaster. Later the same year L B Powell's memorial booklet was published, in association with the Birmingham Central School of Arts and Crafts. Florence Taylor, having sold the Devon house and the pottery, which can be seen in a state of demolition in an aerial photograph taken in 1936, moved back to the United States with her son sometime before 1939. She returned to Britain during the Second World War and probably remained here until the late 1940s.

Interest in the Ruskin Pottery was then eclipsed by world events, but it was briefly revived in July 1947 by an exhibition held at the Great Hampton Street showrooms of Frederick Restall Limited, a well-known Birmingham firm of house furnishers and interior decorators. Over 300 pieces of pottery were on show, drawn from the collections of Florence Taylor and Robert Ferneyhough, and organised by the latter. Indeed, the main purpose of the exhibition seems to have been to show Florence's collection before it was shipped to the United States, to be displayed there as an example of British craftsman-ship. Her collection was certainly taken to America, but it is not known whether the planned exhibition ever took place. When interviewed by James Ruston in the 1960s, Florence said that her collection was still in store in the United States. Since then it seems to have disappeared. When contacted in 1989 her son Harold Atherley had only what he called 'a modest collection', though this did include some first rate pieces of flambé. However, he also had some more personal material, such as the silver centrepiece presented to Edward Taylor when he left Lincoln School of Art, some other commemorative and presentation pieces given to Howson Taylor, and a selection of the medals awarded to Howson Taylor at various national and international exhibitions. His mother's large collection may have been sold previously, Florence having returned to Britain in 1956 or 1957. She then continued to live here until her death in 1973.

In 1955 the *Smethwick Telephone* published two articles by W Ellery Jephcott about the Ruskin Pottery, marking the 20 years that had passed since Taylor's death. These aroused considerable local interest, and were followed by others based on reminiscences by surviving former employees, notably Ernest Porter and William Forrester's wife Sarah Ann. Robert Ferneyhough apart, who bought steadily during the 1950s and 1960s, interest in the Taylors and their pottery then died away again until the 1970s, when a reviving enthusiasm for the British art potters of the late Victorian and Edwardian periods brought Ruskin back to life. Pieces began to appear in the salerooms and a number of general articles were published in art and antiques magazines. The most important, by Ian Bennett, was in the November 1973 issue of *The Connoisseur*. In 1975, 40 years after the pottery's final closure, the Victoria & Albert Museum in London organised a major Ruskin exhibition, drawn solely from the Robert Ferneyhough collection. Subsequently, this formed the basis for a travelling display. The following year Birmingham Museum and Art Gallery mounted an exhibition entitled 'Taylor Made'. This included work by all the Taylor family, and again drew heavily upon the Ferneyhough collection. A further reflection of this burst of Ruskin interest was the publication in 1975 of James Ruston's pioneer study of the pottery, a work based largely on interviews and correspondence in the 1960s with surviving Ruskin employees and their families, and upon documentary material gathered at the time. Other Ruskin books were also under consideration at the time, by L B Powell, Lucien Myers and Robert Ferneyhough himself, but none of these was ever completed. A revised edition of Ruston's invaluable little book was issued in 1990 by Sandwell Metropolitan Borough Council.

Robert Ferneyhough died in 1977, and a gradual dispersal of the Ruskin collection he had received from Howson Taylor then began. An exhibition in 1981 and a series of auction sales have continued the process up to the present day. It is to be hoped that the dispersal of much of the Ferneyhough collection and the publication of this book will together establish permanently the reputation of the Ruskin Pottery and its founders, Edward Richard Taylor and William Howson Taylor. These remarkable men, together with their 'family' of craftsmen and women, upheld for 35 years the aims of good potting, beauty of form and rich or tender colourations. It was their achievement in fulfilling so successfully these simple aims that put the Ruskin Pottery apart from its contemporaries.

William Howson Taylor's granite tombstone, in Ashprington churchyard, Devon.

Appendix I
THE 1905 AND 1906 CATALOGUES OF SHAPES

These illustrations, drawn from the 1905 catalogue, and the revised edition issued in about 1906, show shapes 1-326. It should be noted that by 1906 a number of the 1905 shapes had already been deleted, and so may never have been put into production.

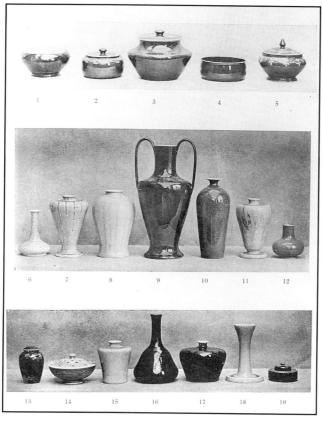

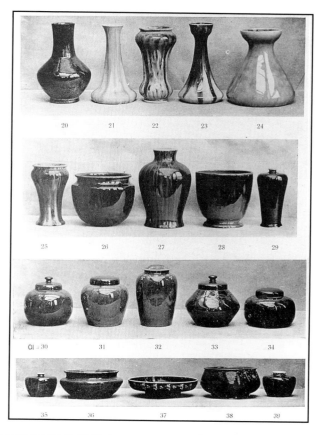

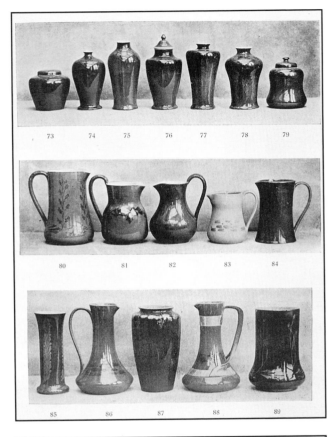

73 74 75 76 77 78 79

80 81 82 83 84

85 86 87 88 89

90 91 92 93 94 95 96

97 98 99 100 101

102 103 104 105 106 107 108

109 110 111 112 113 114 115

116 117 118 119 120 121 122

123 124 125 126 127 128 129 130

131 132 133 134 135 136 137

138 139 140 141 142 143 144 145 146

147 148 149

150 151 152 153 154 155 156 157 158 159 160

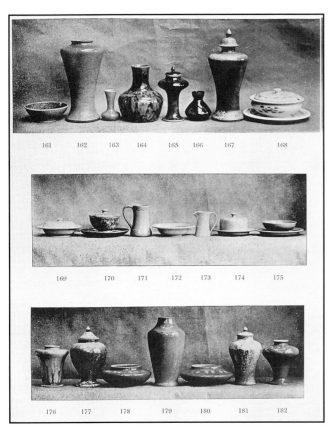

161 162 163 164 165 166 167 168

169 170 171 172 173 174 175

176 177 178 179 180 181 182

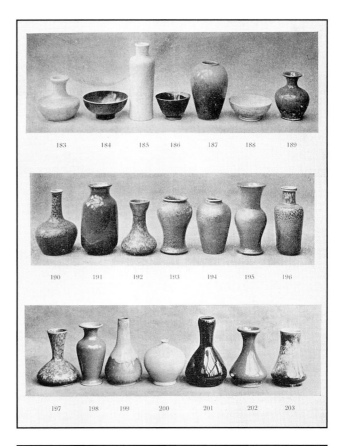

183 184 185 186 187 188 189

190 191 192 193 194 195 196

197 198 199 200 201 202 203

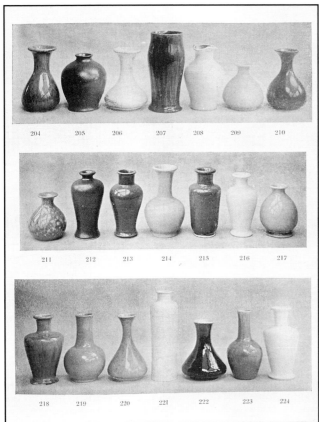

204 205 206 207 208 209 210

211 212 213 214 215 216 217

218 219 220 221 222 223 224

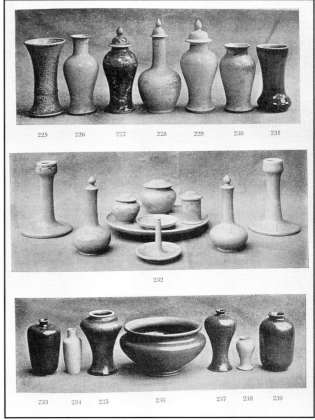

225 226 227 228 229 230 231

232

233 234 235 236 237 238 239

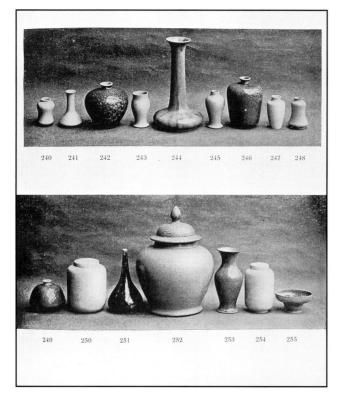

240 241 242 243 244 245 246 247 248

249 250 251 252 253 254 255

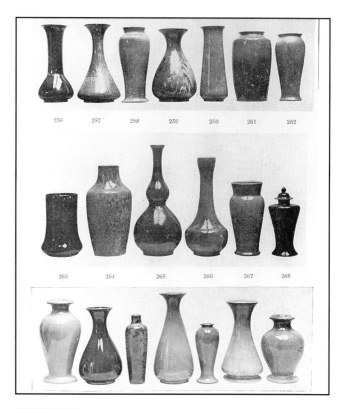

256 257 258 259 260 261 262

263 264 265 266 267 268

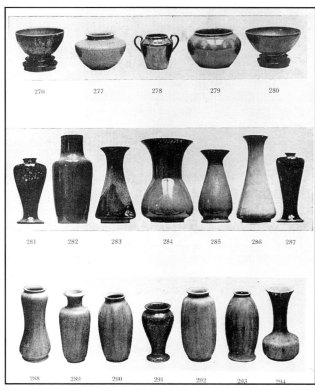

276 277 278 279 280

281 282 283 284 285 286 287

288 289 290 291 292 293 294

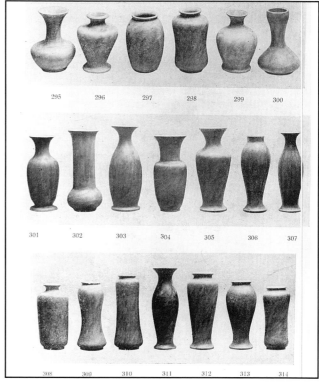

295 296 297 298 299 300

301 302 303 304 305 306 307

308 309 310 311 312 313 314

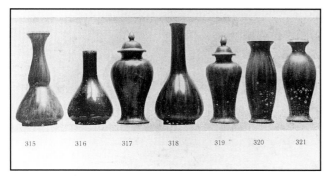

315 316 317 318 319 320 321

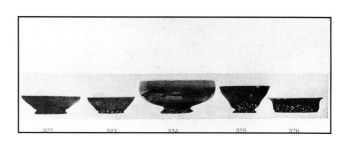

322 323 324 325 326

Appendix II
RUSKIN MARKS AND LABELS

TAYLOR

The impressed TAYLOR mark, sometimes with WEST SMETHWICK added, and occasionally accompanied by a painted scissors mark or impressed shape number, was in use from about 1900 to about 1905.

The impressed WHT monogram mark, for William Howson Taylor, was in use at least from 1901 to about 1905, although examples with later dates are known. It was also used on early stationery.

The scissors mark, usually painted and occasionally scratched, a rebus on the Taylor name, was in use by 1901, and can be found as late as the early 1920s. Often accompanied by other marks.

RUSKIN
POTTERY
WEST SMETHWICK

1908

The impressed oval mark was introduced in 1904 or 1905, and remained in use until 1909. It was often accompanied by an impressed date, from 1905.

RUSKIN   RUSKIN

The standard impressed mark, also occasionally incised or painted, used in various sizes from about 1908.

RUSKIN
POTTERY

WEST SMETHWICK

Impressed mark used from about 1905, initially in a large size, and then smaller from about 1908, often accompanied by an impressed date.

RUSKIN
POTTERY   RUSKIN
POTTERY

Impressed mark used from about 1909 to 1911, in various sizes.

RUSKIN
ENGLAND

Impressed mark used in various sizes from about 1910, usually with an impressed date. From about 1915 this became the standard type of mark. Occasionally it is found painted underglaze, or stamped in black.

RUSKIN

MADE IN ENGLAND

Impressed mark which appears to have been used only in 1922.

RUSKIN
ENGLAND 1933

Impressed triangular mark, used from 1930 to indicate wares turned by Percy Holland.

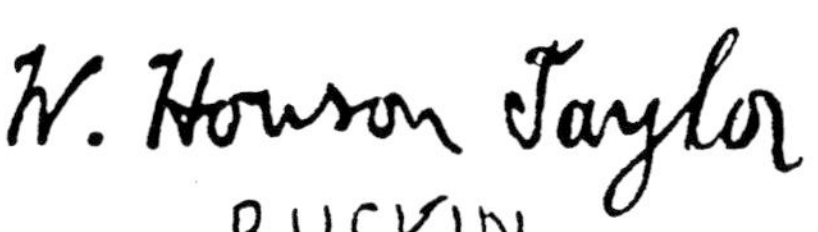

W. Howson Taylor
RUSKIN
ENGLAND

The incised or painted signature of Howson Taylor can be found on a range of wares from 1930 to 1933, combined with an impressed mark and date.

Raised mark used on some late moulded wares.

Other recorded marks include shape numbers and experimental glaze numbers.

LABELS

The Taylors made use over a long period of a wide range of paper labels designed to be attached to the base of the ware. The earliest were in use at least by 1905, and the latest by the mid-1920s. Many were particularly associated with flambé and other high temperature glazes. The selection shown here is in approximate date order.

THIS PIECE OF
RUSKIN POTTERY
CANNOT
BE REPEATED.

RUSKIN POTTERY
This colour scheme
cannot be repeated.

Ruskin Pottery.
GRAND PRIZE, ST. LOUIS.

Ruskin Pottery.
GRAND PRIZE, MILAN.
GRAND PRIZE, ST. LOUIS.
"HORS CONCOURS,"
CHRISTCHURCH,
NEW ZEALAND, 1907.
No. | Price
K

Ruskin Pottery.
LEADLESS GLAZE.
No | Price
20 | X

Ruskin Pottery.
LEADLESS GLAZE.
No. | Price
374. | £0.

KNOWN EXHIBITIONS OF RUSKIN POTTERY

1901, Smethwick Municipal School of Art

1902, October, 5th Exhibition of the Bristol and Clifton Arts and Crafts Society

1903, January, 7th display by the London Arts and Crafts Exhibition Society

June, Arts and Crafts Exhibition at Alexandra Palace, London

1904, January, Exhibition at the Woodbury Gallery

June, Arts and Crafts Exhibition, Port Sunlight

August, Louisiana Purchase International Exposition, St Louis, USA. Ruskin Pottery's 1st Grand Prix Award

August, Leicester Arts and Crafts Exhibition

September, Arts and Crafts Exhibition, Leeds City Art Gallery

October (?), Loan Exhibition of British Pottery and Porcelain, Glasgow

1905, February, Arts and Crafts Exhibition, Leeds City Art Gallery

May, 21st annual exhibition, Home Arts and Industries Association. First of many Ruskin displays at this event

November, Arts and Crafts Exhibition, Bruton Galleries, London

1906, January, 8th display by the London Arts and Crafts Exhibition Society, at Grafton Gallery

Esposizione Internationale Milano, Italy. Ruskin Pottery's 2nd Grand Prix Award

1907, Exhibition of China and Earthenware Finished with Leadless Glaze, Church House, London

International Exhibition, Christchurch, New Zealand. 'Hors Concours' Award

Autumn, Home Arts and Industries Association, Albert Hall, London

1908, May, Franco-British Exhibition, White City, London. Ruskin Pottery's 3rd Grand Prix Award

Autumn, Ideal Home Exhibition, London

1909, July, Imperial International Exhibition, White City, London

1909 International Exhibition, Venice, Italy

September, *Modern English Pottery*, Queen's Park branch, Manchester City Art Gallery

1910, February, 9th display by the London Arts and Crafts Exhibition Society

April, International Competition in Artistic Pottery

Exposition Universelle de Bruxelles, Belgium. Ruskin Pottery awarded two Grand Prix

Ideal Home Exhibition, London

1911, Empire and Imperial Exhibition, Crystal Palace, London

International Exhibition, Turin, Italy. Ruskin Pottery awarded Grand Prix

1912, November, 10th display by the London Arts and Crafts Exhibition Society

1913, Arts and Crafts Exhibition, Grosvenor Gallery, London

Ideal Home Exhibition, London

Exposition Universelle et Internationale, Ghent, Belgium. Ruskin Pottery awarded Grand Prix

1914, May, Cambridge Arts and Crafts Society

1915, British Industries Fair. First of many Ruskin displays at this annual event

1916, British Industries Fair

November, 11th display by the London Arts and Crafts Exhibition Society

1917, Autumn, Special display by the London Arts and Crafts Exhibition Society

1920, June, *Modern Crafts and Manufactures*, 1st exhibition by British Institute of Industrial Art, Knightsbridge, London

1921, British Institute of Industrial Art, London

1922, British Institute of Industrial Art, London

1923, 12th display by the London Arts and Crafts Exhibition Society, Royal Academy, London

September, *Industrial Art of Today*, exhibition by British Institute of Industrial Art, Knightsbridge, London

September, *Recent Examples of British Pottery*, Victoria & Albert Museum, London

1924, April, British Empire Exhibition, Wembley, London

December, British Institute of Industrial Art, Whitworth Institute, Manchester

December, Applied Arts and Handicrafts Exhibition, Royal Agricultural Hall, London

1925, April, Exposition Internationale des Arts Décoratifs et Industriels Modernes, Paris, France

September, Artist Potters Exhibition, Heal & Sons, London

December, Applied Arts and Handicrafts Exhibition, Royal Agricultural Hall, London

1926, January, 13th display by the London Arts and Crafts Exhibition Society

March, British Industries Fair, White City, London

June, Applied Arts and Handicrafts Exhibition, Royal Agricultural Hall, London

Sesquicentennial International Exhibition, Philadelphia, USA

July, Ruskin Gallery, Birmingham

November, Home Arts and Industries Association, Drapers Hall, London

December, Applied Arts and Handicrafts Exhibition, Royal Agricultural Hall, London

1927, British Industries Fair

1929, Arts and Crafts Fair, Leipzig, Germany

1930, May, International Exhibition of Decorative and Industrial Art, Monza, Italy

1933, June, *Industrial Art in Relation to the Home*, exhibition by British Institute of Industrial Art, Dorland Hall, London

International Exhibition of Decorative Art, Milan, Italy

1934, January, Ruskin Gallery, Birmingham and Loan Exhibition, Birmingham Art Gallery

1936, February, Memorial Exhibition, Ruskin Gallery, Birmingham

1947, July, Exhibition of Ruskin from Taylor and Ferneyhough family collections, Frederick Restall Ltd, Birmingham

1952, *Victorian and Edwardian Decorative Art*, Victoria & Albert Museum, London

1975, October, Ruskin pottery from the Ferneyhough collection, Victoria & Albert Museum, London. A smaller version subsequently travelled around other museums in Britain

1976, *Taylor Made* exhibition, Birmingham Museum and Art Gallery

1981, Ruskin Pottery from the Ferneyhough collection, Haslam and Whiteway, London

Some British Museums with Ruskin Collections

Bedford, Cecil Higgins Museum

Birmingham, Museum and Art Gallery

Brighton, Museum and Art Gallery

Bristol, Museum and Art Gallery

Glasgow, Museum and Art Gallery

Leicester, Museum and Art Gallery

Liverpool, Museum and Art Gallery

London, Victoria & Albert Museum

Manchester, City Art Gallery

Nottingham, Castle Museum

Stoke-on-Trent, City Museum and Art Gallery

Wednesbury, Art Gallery and Museum

BIBLIOGRAPHY

Selected Background Literature

1873, *Histoire de la Céramique*, A Jacquemart, Paris. English translation published 1877

1887, *La Faience*, T Deck, Paris

1894, 'The Renaissance of the Potter's Art in France', *The Studio*, vol 3, London (perhaps by Charles Haviland)

1895, *Blue and White Oriental Porcelain*, C Monkhouse and R Mills, The Burlington Fine Arts Club, London

1896, *Oriental Ceramic Art*, S W Bushell, 10 vols, New York
Coloured Porcelain, Cosmo Monkhouse and R Mills, The Burlington Fine Arts Club, London

1897, *The Manual of Practical Potting*, edited C F Binns
Ceramic Technololgy, C F Binns

1898, *Chinese Porcelain*, W G Gulland, London
Researches on Leadless Glazes, W J Furnival, Staffordshire

1901, *History and Description of Chinese Porcelain*, C Monkhouse, London

1902, *Collected Works of Hermann Seger*, edited A Bleininger, Pennsylvania
History and Description of English Porcelain, W Burton, London

1904, 'Crystalline Glazes and their Application to the Decoration of Pottery', W Burton, *Journal of the Royal Society of Arts*, vol LII, London
Leadless Decorative Tiles, Faience and Mosaic, W J Furnival, Staffordshire

1905, *Grand Feu Ceramics*, T Doat, USA

1910, *Early Chinese Pottery and Porcelain*, The Burlington Fine Arts Club, London

1916, 'Notes on Some Chinese Glazes on Pottery and Porcelain', J N Collie, *Transactions of the English Ceramic Society*, London

1921/2, 'Monograph on the Copper Red Glazes', J N Collie, *Transactions of the Oriental Ceramic Society*, London

1927, *Guide to the Later Chinese Porcelains*, W B Honey, London

1976, *Ernest Chaplet*, J d'Albis, Paris

1980, *Pilkington's Royal Lancastrian Pottery and Tiles*, A J Cross, London

1982, *Bernard Moore Master Potter 1850-1936*, A Dawson, London

1984, 'The Copper Red Glazes with Particular Reference to the Work of Bernard Moore', D A Hall, PhD thesis, Manchester Polytechnic

Literature Relating to the Ruskin Pottery

1890, *Elementary Art Teaching, An Educational and Technical Guide for Teachers and Learners*, E R Taylor, London

1893, *Textbook on Drawing and Design for Beginners*, E R Taylor, London

1894, 'Mr E R Taylor; Edgbastonians Past and Present', *Edgbastonia* vol XIV, Birmingham

1901, 'Ruskin Pottery', *The Artist*, December, pp 208-9

1904, 'Ruskin Pottery', J A Service, *American Pottery Gazette*
'Lessons from the St Louis Exhibition', C F Binns, *Transactions of the American Ceramic Society*, vol VII

1905, *Art Journal*, article and illustration, p 383

1908, 'British Pottery', J A Service, *Art Journal*, pp 53-7, 129-37, 238-44 (3 articles)
Illustrated Review of the 1908 Franco-British Exhibition, edited F G Dumas, London

1911, 'Some Modern Pottery', H M Pemberton, *Art Journal*, pp 119-26

1913, *A Notable Art Master*, Kate Hall, Birmingham

1923, 'W Howson Taylor, Men and Women of Today', *World's Work*, March, vol XLI, no 244

1936, *Howson Taylor Master Potter*, L B Powell, Central School of Arts and Crafts, Birmingham

1973, 'Ruskin Pottery', I Bennett, *The Connoisseur*, November, pp 180-5

1974, 'Chinese Influence on Ruskin Pottery', L B Powell, *Antique Dealer and Collectors Guide*, January, pp 78-80

1975, *Ruskin Pottery*, J H Ruston, Metropolitan Borough of Sandwell
Ruskin Pottery from the Ferneyhough Collection, catalogue of the Victoria & Albert Museum exhibition

1976, *British Art Pottery 1870-1940*, A W Coysh, London
'Edward R Taylor and the Birmingham Municipal School of Art', R Hartnell, MA thesis, Royal College of Art

1980, *A Edward Jones Metalcraftsman*, G Wild, Museum and Art Gallery, Birmingham

1981, *Ruskin Pottery, A Selection from the Ferneyhough Collection*, I Bennett, catalogue of exhibition at Haslam & Whiteway, London

1984, *By Hammer and Hand, The Arts and Crafts Movement in Birmingham*, edited Alan Crawford, Museum and Art Gallery, Birmingham

1990, *Ruskin Pottery*, J H Ruston, revised and expanded edition, Sandwell Metropolitan Borough Council

Major Magazine and Newspaper References

The Studio

1904, October, review of Leicester Arts and Crafts exhibition, with illustration, vol 33, pp 81-2

1905, March, review of Arts and Crafts exhibition, Leeds Art Gallery, vol 33, p 353

1906, January, Birmingham Studio Talk and illustration, vol 36, pp 357-8
May, Review of London Arts and Crafts exhibition, vol 37
September, review of Milan international exhibition, vol 38, p 301

1925, November, illustrated Ruskin advertisement, New High Temperature Flambé Ware, vol 90, p 392

1926, March, review of the London Arts and Crafts exhibition, vol 91, p 396

1926 June, review with 5 photographs of Ruskin Gallery exhibition

The Studio Yearbook of Decorative Art

1907, text page 161, illustration p 163

1908, article and illustration

1909, illustration p 120

1910, illustration p 141

1913, illustrations p 112

1915, text p 129, illustration p 154

1916, text p 58, illustration p 81

1917, illustration p 100

1927, illustration p 135

1928, illustration p 159

1929, illustration p 182

1930, illustration p 168

The *Pottery Gazette* and *Glass Trades Review*

Between January 1903 and October 1935 the *Pottery Gazette* regularly contained material relevant to the Ruskin Pottery. Listed below are some of the more important entries:

1903, January, general article on the pottery
April, review of London Arts and Crafts exhibition

1905, November, description of the 1905 catalogue

1906, February, review of the St Louis exhibition
April, review of the London Arts and Crafts exhibition

1907, November, report of Edward Taylor's speech at the opening of the new Burslem School of Art

1908, August, review of the Franco-British exhibition
December, review and illustration of the Ideal Home exhibition

1909, June, review of the Venice International exhibition

1910, August, review of the Brussels exhibition
November, illustration of Brussels display

1911, July, review of Turin exhibition

1912, February, obituary of Edward Taylor

1915, June, review of the British Industries Fair
       July, general article on the pottery with
       illustration

1917, April, general article including description of
       new brochure with illustration

1924, July, review of the Wembley exhibition
       September, description of the new brochure

1925, September, review of the Paris exhibition
       with illustration

1926, May, illustration of wares presented to
       Birmingham Museum

1928, February, general article on the pottery with
       illustration

1932, February, general article on the pottery with
       illustrations

1933, July, review of Dorland Hall exhibition
       December, notice of factory closure

1935, November, obituary of Howson Taylor

Other newspapers

Birmingham Daily Post

1903, 29th June, retirement of Edward Taylor

1933, 30th December, notice of factory closure

1935, 26th September, obituary of Howson Taylor

1968, 23rd December, article on Ruskin by
       L B Powell

Birmingham Gazette

1930, 4th April, 'Potter's Art at Smethwick', photo-
       feature

1930, 29th July, illustrated article in series
       'Romances of Midland Industries'

1934, 21st December, illustrated article, 'Smethwick
       Man Refuses to Accept Fortune for a Secret'

Birmingham Mail

1935, 25th September, obituary of Howson Taylor

Smethwick Telephone

1934, April, 'A Famous West Smethwick Pottery'

1955, 20th May, 27th May, 8th July, general articles
       on the pottery, with staff reminiscences

Evening Despatch

1933, 13th December, notice of closure

1934, 11th January, review of 1934 Ruskin Gallery
       exhibition